In Praise of *Qoheleth,* THE TEACHER / *Qoheleth,* MY MUSE

"Should you choose to accompany poet Deborah Lynn Dalton (d²) on her journey through the 'wisdom literature' of the Old Testament Book of Ecclesiastes, be sure to bring your own shoes designed to withstand tough terrain, desert hotspots, ebbing tides, unexpected curves and sudden drops. Be prepared for blood smears, heart-defying leaps with craterous landings, grief and a sense of foreloneness not backed up with hope. Be prepared for foolishness disguised as nothing new under the sun, threatening one's perceived wisdom and capability to make any sense or success of the abbreviated time afforded one on earth. Time, that is experienced as a vapor or hebel that temporarily fills a space and then dissipates without announcement or fanfare. Ecclesiastes is serious business, as is our Poet Dalton, who has welcomed The Teacher, Qoheleth, as her Muse."

—Reverend Adrienne L. Phillips, Charlotte, North Carolina, M.Div, M.Ed, M.S., Poet, Preacher, Servant, Teacher

"Her call…one to move the masses with words, wisdom, insight, healing, and love. Her example…one that makes an imprint you never want to erase. Her words…a balm for a world troubled, disturbed, fragmented and in need of reconcile. Thank God for the life of Deborah d² Dalton!

You don't have to study Hebrew, like I did once upon a time, to receive the rich value in this collection of poems, prose, welcoming words, and what I call 'wisdom nuggets.' What you do have to do is have an open heart, mind and spirit to receive ancient and modern mysteries revealed via the prayers and outpourings of our Dearest Deborah. Be prepared for transformation as you indulge in the book of Ecclesiastes like you have never witnessed before. This work made me 'examine my existence/ a philosophical conundrum/ questioning if I am really and truly here.' (An excerpt from the poem Wisdom Invites Madness.)

Reading Qoheleth, THE TEACHER / Qoheleth, MY MUSE took me on a spiritual journey to become whole that I will revisit every time I AM in need of healing, reconciliation, and remembering."

—Reverend Iyana "Yani" Davis, M.Div., Founder, The Peace People's Movement

"In this brilliant literary piece, Deborah, d². has invited us to join her in a stroll through the botanical garden called Ecclesiastes. Equipped with a theological and literary green thumb, she has tilled the soil of this ancient work of wisdom, and coaxed fresh and new perspectives for our mind's eyes to gaze, ponder, contemplate, consider, and appreciate.

As you stroll through this treasured garden with Deborah as your guide, I assure you, you will see this ancient, biblical book of poetry and wisdom in a new light. Thank you, d², for allowing the Spirit to birth in you a new way to view and appreciate an old, oft neglected literary jewel: Ecclesiastes.

PS: To Deborah, thanks for introducing us to Fran…"

—**Reverend Dr. Gregory K. Moss, Sr., Pastor Emeritus, St. Paul Baptist Church, Charlotte, NC, Interim Pastor, Chapell Memorial Baptist Church.**

Qoheleth, THE TEACHER
Qoheleth, MY MUSE

Qoheleth, THE TEACHER
Qoheleth, MY MUSE

Poems About Poems

by d²

A Poetic Commentary

World Stage Press
Verse from the Village

@d2poetry / @worldstagepress

World Stage Press
Verse from the Village

QOHELETH, THE TEACHER / QOHELETH, MY MUSE: Poems About Poems
© 2024 Deborah Lynn Dalton, 1-347402058

ISBN: 978-1-952952-57-9

Cover art, "No, Not Every Poem Ends in Redemption"
© 2016, Deborah Lynn Dalton

Photography throughout, From the Series: "A Quiet Hour for Michelle"
© 2022, Deborah Lynn Dalton, Buckroe Beach, Hampton, VA

First Edition, 2024

All rights reserved. No part of this publication may be reproduced, distributed, or transmitted in any form or by any means, including photocopying, recording, or other electronic or mechanical methods, without the prior written permission of the publisher, except in the case of brief quotations embodied in critical reviews and certain other noncommercial uses permitted by copyright law.

Author website: d-sqrd.com
Publisher website: worldstagepress.org

Scripture taken from the Holy Bible, New International Version®, NIV®. Copyright© 1973, 1978, 1984, 2011 by Biblica, Inc.™ Used by permission of Zondervan. All rights reserved worldwide. www.zondervan.com". "The "NIV" and "New International Version" are trademarks registered in the United States Patent and Trademark Offices by Biblica, Inc.™.

Scripture quotations marked "NKJV" are taken from the New King James Version®. Copyright © 1982 by Thomas Nelson. Used by permission. All rights reserved.

"so, i became" was originally published in the book *Becoming Aware.*, ISBN-13: 979-8-218-35292-9

"Wisdom Invites Madness" was originally published in *The 2017 Poetry Marathon Anthology*, edited by Caitlin Jans, published by Authors Publish Press, Nov. 25, 2017., ISBN-10: 1942344031, ISBN-13: 978-1942344032

Printed in the United States of America

Edited by Brooke Feichti and Ghislane LeFranc
Cover Design by Deborah Lynn Dalton and Emily Anne Evans
Layout Design by Deborah Lynn Dalton and Christa Varley

To my penultimate cheerleaders:

Daddy, you taught me the power and peace of contentment while clinging to a bucket list undone.

You were the perfect father, for me.

Momma, you opened my soul to the wonders of creativity throughout your life and taught me the power of community through your death.

You were the perfect mother, for me.

Qoheleth, THE TEACHER
Qoheleth, MY MUSE

Forewords

Reverend Dr. Robert C. Scott

The writings of Sister Deborah Dalton on the musings and insights of Solomon in Ecclesiastes are filled with the trials and travails of being an African American woman in times like these. The layers of womanism synthesized with the sagacity of King Solomon is raised to a 21st-century rendering of appreciating the limitations of human achievements, which tends to be cast to the wayside by future generations. As Solomon pens insights about how the pursuit of the material is rather vain, how the wicked seems to get away with unrighteousness, and combating injustice is rather futile, we are encouraged in his writings to be satisfied with our lot in life.

Deborah offers the reader another perspective which is birthed through the intersectionality of her being a Black/African American, single woman who has experienced the highs and lows of reality which forge her theopoetic offerings. Because of her race, class, and gender in a country and a world that does not really provide the appreciation of the Divine, Deborah's offering gives us insights and inspiration using Ecclesiastes as a backdrop to deal with the marginalization, disenfranchisement, and oppression encountered by Black/African American women in particular—and by all sinners in general. The "simplexity"—taking the complex and making it simple—of the theological poetry should give one strength in the struggle for justice, freedom, personal agency, humanity, and divinity as Black women are reminded how they, too, are created in the image and likeness of God.

As you read her musings, you will appreciate how Deborah reflects on various strands of life, learnings, legacy, and light to the rhythms of the Creator imposed upon her soul. Read and drink deeply from her words and her engagement with the supposedly wisest king of Israel. You will discover who is really wise in this rendering.

The Reverend Dr. Robert Charles Scott, Senior Pastor
St. Paul Baptist Church
Charlotte, North Carolina
May 2023

Reverend Dr. Jeremiah A. Wright, Jr.

Minister Deborah Dalton has written an amazingly important work for believers and nonbelievers alike. Following the lead of Qoheleth, who wrote the Book of Ecclesiastics based on his own experiences, Sister Dalton has written an important "commentary" based on her own experiences paralleling passages of Qoheleth's writing.

Ms. Dalton's writing draws the reader into the inner sanctum of her soul and evokes a visceral response to every page of this text. Her masterful use of the English language, her artful creation of new phrases heretofore unseen, and the passion of her life's experiences are all wrapped up into a volume that you will not want to put down once you start reading it!

Take, for instance, the phrase "climbing down" the stairs. That is but one of at least a hundred turns of phrase that make this poetry more than poetry.

Ms. Dalton's masterful blending of onomatopoeia, homophones, alliteration. and deep spiritual insight of the journey God has led her on makes for incredibly delightful reading. Closing this volume with moving tributes to her mother and father, who are both with the Lord, Ms. Dalton has indeed "clicked her heels" and returned home, leaving the reader gasping for breath and wanting more!

I take objection to what Ms. Dalton said in her introduction, however. She says she is not a preacher. She accepted her call to ministry after having run for such a long time because she knew that preaching was not her divine call or divine purpose.

Walt Whitman coined the phrase. Walter Brueggemann uses the phrase for his definition of prophetic preaching. I say, however, that the phrase "finally comes a poet" is why I disagree with Ms. Dalton.

Brueggemann argues accurately that the true preacher or prophet who tells forth the Word of God and makes plain for the reader or the hearer the heart of God is in the final analysis a poet. Brueggemann could have been writing about Deborah Dalton when he said, "Finally comes the poet!" This work demonstrates how she is indeed a preacher, showing us the mind of God and the will of a holy God for the human community made lovingly in God's image, *imago Dei*.

The poetry in this volume is more than poetry. It is the heart of God made plain for those "who have ears." There is found in these lines of inspired poetry God's vision for the reader and God's love for the world!

The emotions spanning in this one volume cover a vast range of human experiences, from divinely given love to the horror of rape. The trauma of human experiences is balanced out in this volume by Ms. Dalton's giving the reader a glimpse of God's glory, giving divinely inspired commentary—as did Qoheleth.

This is such an important addendum to the "corpus of commentaries" on Ecclesiastes that I would dare to say if you open your heart to be touched by Ms. Dalton's heart in this volume, the heart of an African American woman born in the 20th Century ("I am a Negro!"), your life will never be the same.

Reverend Dr. Jeremiah A. Wright, Jr.
Pastor Emeritus
Trinity United Church of Christ
Chicago, Illinois
May 2023

Qoheleth, THE TEACHER
Qoheleth, MY MUSE

Poems About Poems

INTRODUCTION

My call.

I remember my call to ministry.

Mind you, this resolute understanding came after decades of denial fueled by social norms and self-doubt. But the call chased me long enough until I stopped and embraced it as my own.

It was a humbling calmness that called me out of the languishing mediocrity of a secular vocation I detested without ever knowing why.

At once, I understood and lamented the time "wasted" to get to this point. But what did it mean? What was my next step?

Each Christian denomination has a slightly different process to affirm and develop the context of a "call," but what I knew to be true existed somewhere outside of man-made constraints of what it should be.

What I know for sure is that I am a poet. I know that I have a sincere heart to serve God and God's people. And I know that my life seems to rattle between the pages of Ecclesiastes.

And, although I have the gift of gab, I am almost certain that this call is not for me to be a preacher.

I am a poet with a desire to serve.

I think each person has a scripture that deeply resonates with them, almost like the designated theme music from a blaxploitation film. Mine was, and is, Ecclesiastes 1:2, "Meaningless! Meaningless!" says the Teacher. "Utterly meaningless! Everything is meaningless." These words stumped me. "Meaningless..." "Everything..." Really?

The more I fought against embracing this scripture, the more my life proved its message to be true, in a secular, hopeless fashion. So, I sought to flip the script. I decided to dig into this entire book and prayerfully seek what God inspired me to craft as poetic interpretation, and then convey the narrative of the impact of this text on my life.

This was a quest to wrestle with: "What does it mean to matter?" "Where do we find redemption?" And "What are the themes in life that are consistently repeated by us all?"

This book is a culmination of more than 22 years of study and writing—and, has proven to be one of the most enlightening processes of my life. This book required that I live each pericope before I could write. I am still living them. I will be living them until the final closing of my eyes.

Reading, meditating, researching, praying, and then writing about this text has revealed how we matter is when we are unabashedly affirmed in our identity and experiences, true redemption is our source of sincere joy, and all of humanity shares a common thematic desire to seek meaning within a construct that we must first strip away its oppressive meaning for all of us to become whole.

Prologue

#OurLivesMatter

Ecclesiastes 1-2

Absent a true connection to Christ we are unable to discern what is truly substantive about our existence. We get caught up in defining ourselves with things of transient value, things that are mired in labels of varying importance, battling for prominence in a world that touts hierarchy as supreme. What truly matters is obscured by the assertion that what concerns the individual matters most. But it is through annihilating the desire to matter that we are prepared to fully appreciate the beauty of Christ at work. This is then the work that we endeavor to co-labor beside him, and how we are to ultimately define our worth.

The Book of Ecclesiastes, Chapter 1

Can I see a thing in its sanitized is-ness outside of my experience birthed in my opinions tainted by my personal brand of celebrated wisdom?

Can I see it clean?

9.24.22, "Water Without Borders"

As Qoheleth Admires the Sun

Ecclesiastes 1:1-2

[1] *The words of the Teacher, son of David, king in Jerusalem:*

[2] *"Meaningless! Meaningless!"*
  says the Teacher.
"Utterly meaningless!
  Everything is meaningless."

Captured in its rays
our essence
coalesces
in like manner
stretching to
capture
new breaths
contracting with
heartbeats
silenced
leaving a temple
structure
staid
strong
sure
foundation secure
while shifting blocks
of a puzzle
already solved
just absent
coordinating colors
in awe
seeing
the beauty of
forms already

complex layers
pulled to reveal
what is needed
to coordinate a
re-lived fixture

Ecclesiastes 1:1-2

amazing,
it is,
this Organism
birthed for eternal
purpose
which will only
manifest
once this temporal
embryonic
viscous film
is ruptured.

~ d², 08.05.17, 9:26 AM

Overwhelm

Spinning plates

deadlines chasing
last seconds of the day

the stale wind slapped
by the ticking second hand

anxious heart
heavy head

no room to start
no space to end

~ d², 06.26.21, 5:15 PM

Ecclesiastes 1:3-7

*³ What do people gain from
all their labors
   at which they toil under the sun?*

*⁴ Generations come and generations go,
   but the earth remains forever.*

*⁵ The sun rises and the sun sets,
   and hurries back to where it rises.*

*⁶ The wind blows to the south
   and turns to the north;
round and round it goes,
   ever returning on its course.*

*⁷ All streams flow into the sea,
   yet the sea is never full.
To the place the streams come from,
   there they return again.*

Ecclesiastes 1:8-11

*⁸ All things are wearisome,
  more than one can say.
The eye never has enough of seeing,
  nor the ear its fill of hearing.*

*⁹ What has been will be again,
  what has been done will be done again;
  there is nothing new under the sun.*

*¹⁰ Is there anything of which one can say,
  "Look! This is something new"?
It was here already, long ago;
  it was here before our time.*

*¹¹ No one remembers the former generations,
  and even those yet to come
will not be remembered
  by those who follow them.*

The Unheard Melody

Restless

Aching

Energy

Craving

outlets to relieve
monuments of
pent-up stirrings

recoiling chaotically

seeking language
unrehearsed

before I step on stage

to say
or convey
aortic texts
from heart
to head

bowing to
accolades
it wrenches my waist
squeezing training

stabilizing correcting

Ecclesiastes 1:8-11

I am ignorant
to the wisdom
it must possess

naïve to this
longing

warming to the
idea of
conforming to
a reality that
I highly
respect

will it acknowledge
the itinerant
presence of my
labored breath

staccato measures
abate a rumbling
explosion
imploding
torrential
storming
forming
swarming
transforming

catalogs of
considerations
bereft

Ecclesiastes 1:8-11

of warning
that alarm is
sounding

danger is
in the new morning

or abandoned
in the past

gripping apprehension
resolute with
regret

prophetically
revealing an
awkward retelling
of novels set
in an
illusionary
past

but I have this
itch
to be
scratched
with nails
evoking trails of
raised
heated
abrasions
sincere tracks of

Ecclesiastes 1:8-11

trains traveled
on a journey

skipping rose petals
in the path

bare toes on
steaming asphalt
bounce
tender and scraped
cooled
with
aloe salve

almost a
satisfying
substitution
for a
firm and gentle
guiding hand
warmly placed
on the
small of my
back.

~ d^2, 04.18.15, 10:20 PM

Ecclesiastes 1:1-11

¹*The words of the Teacher, son of David, king in Jerusalem:*

²*"Meaningless! Meaningless!"*
  says the Teacher.
"Utterly meaningless!
  Everything is meaningless."

³*What do people gain from all their labors*
  at which they toil under the sun?

⁴*Generations come and generations go,*
  but the earth remains forever.

⁵*The sun rises and the sun sets,*
  and hurries back to where it rises.

⁶*The wind blows to the south*
  and turns to the north;
round and round it goes,
  ever returning on its course.

⁷*All streams flow into the sea,*
  yet the sea is never full.
To the place the streams come from,
  there they return again.

⁸*All things are wearisome,*
  more than one can say.

The eye never has enough of seeing,
  nor the ear its fill of hearing.

⁹*What has been will be again,*
  what has been done will be done again;
    there is nothing new under the sun.

An Uncomfortable Truth

Cycles have
a dwindling
vortex to pointless
like a
regenerative fuel
depleting its abundance
as sunsets
shrink and expand
between
measured moments
draining batteries that
paralyze clock hands

Toils have limits
on how often
they are spent
crushing bones
by the labor
of exhaustion

Supporting
the spectrum from
slaps toward
grasps
of infantile
breathing
to
eulogizing
pine-boxed
unclenched
embraces
exhaled

This is the antithesis of
enlightenment

Meanwhile
laughter subsides
as the comedy
grows stale
left to search for
joy in the mourning
awarding trophies
of grieving
monuments
of memories
so precious
evaporating
dehydrating
weeping
to a dusty residue

Remains

to blow
to casually
disappearing into

      a   care fr e e

                v a p o r

~ d², 06.13.15, 12:08 AM

Ecclesiastes 1:1-11

[10]*Is there anything of which one can say,*
   "Look! This is something new"?
It was here already, long ago;
   it was here before our time.

[11]*No one remembers the former generations,*
   and even those yet to come
will not be remembered
   by those who follow them.

Ecclesiastes 1:12-14

[12] I, the Teacher, was king over Israel in Jerusalem. [13] I applied my mind to study and to explore by wisdom all that is done under the heavens. What a heavy burden God has laid on mankind! [14] I have seen all the things that are done under the sun; all of them are meaningless, a chasing after the wind.

To Be Shift-Less

I shift
often by whim and fleeting fancy
through moments
conspired to fend off frustrations
conflicts where
I am at the affect of the
consequences of
ill-conceived choices,
sparked by the whims indulged before

I tread water, drowning
doing the death count
down
seeking unprepared life rafts
in the middle of the oceans
of my own design
choppy waters ginned up
by the currents of the whirlwinds of
a flippant mind

If I could just learn
to take a beat
pause or retreat,
until my purpose guides
not my meaningless entitled mind

I would see clearly the ties that bind
and ease into my righteous
unique, glorious, and
ambitious comfort

~ d^2, 10.01.22, 10:27 PM

Release

In conclusion
I release
shed
remove
dispose and cleanse

bring out the sage and burn it in each room

rinse off the crystal and wrap it in silk

remove this filth

cut the locks, dreads, or curls
shave the head

clear out the closet of left-behind threads

if we could only burn the bed

delete and block
unfriend

drop the weight
like lead

they are now ghosts
the walking dead

~ d², 06.25.22, 2:18 PM

Ecclesiastes 1:15-17

[15] *What is crooked cannot be straightened;
what is lacking cannot be counted.*

[16] *I said to myself, "Look, I have increased in wisdom more than anyone who has ruled over Jerusalem before me; I have experienced much of wisdom and knowledge."*

[17] *Then I applied myself to the understanding of wisdom, and also of madness and folly, but I learned that this, too, is a chasing after the wind.*

Ecclesiastes 1:18

[18] For with much wisdom comes much sorrow;
  the more knowledge, the more grief.

Reconciling the Smoke

Where...

The Sage ponders

The Stage swallows

The Ensemble
casts surreal shadows

The Actors standing translucent
between curtain calls

The Audience showers
accolades for repeated bows
calls for encores
oblivious to
backstage prop falls
dropped lines or missed cues

but once exposed
what is only destroyed
regardless of a
powerful
performance
is just a useless
illusion

~ d^2, 08.05.17, 10:14 AM

The Book of Ecclesiastes, Chapter 2

She balanced her life into equal compartments. Colorful shanties ready to house her varying definitions of family.

9.24.22, "Shacks in a Row"

The Pointless Promise

I...

I...

I...

I wish that I could expertly paint a picture that evoked an emotion so guttural that when those who gaze upon its visage, a reluctant tear of bittersweet melancholy would carelessly fall

But that would be meaningless

I wish that I could energetically inhale, filling up my lungs, topping them off with an up-to-capacity sigh like the soothing aroma of candle wax lazily melting —expressing its hypnotic fragrant throw immediately infusing through my pores into every one of my beckoning cells the joy that it promises

But that would be meaningless

I wish my third glass of IPA would wrap a jovial buzz around my shoulders, escort me gently upstairs, and neatly tuck me into my bed, coaxing dreams of fulfillment, sparking a contentment that would seat me firmly in complete eternal peace

But that would be meaningless

I wish that the way I could nestle into awaiting arms, melting into the intricate architecture of a side that would comfort me with the need to be fully seen

Ecclesiastes 2:1-3

[2] I said to myself, "Come now, I will test you with pleasure to find out what is good." But that also proved to be meaningless. [2] "Laughter," I said, "is madness. And what does pleasure accomplish?" [3] I tried cheering myself with wine, and embracing folly—my mind still guiding me with wisdom. I wanted to see what was good for people to do under the heavens during the few days of their lives.

Ecclesiastes 2:1-3

But that would be meaningless

It is all meaningless

Whether or not I lose these last 50 pounds

It is meaningless

Whether or not I buy myself the perfectly appointed new house

It is meaningless

Whether or not I finally organize all my stuff in its own anointed spot

It is meaningless

Whether or not this sniffling from my incessant allergies stops

It is meaningless

Whether or not I complete this endless list of tasks, filling up my note pads and computer-generated reminders

It is meaningless

Whether or not I ever achieve another damn orgasm

It is meaningless

Ecclesiastes 2:1-3

And I sigh

As I wrestle with the potential of each experience, each possibility in a world full of promise as a gift to those who are living

Those who seek to prove that they are fully alive

I sigh

I moan

I stretch out my muscles to waken them from rest or pull them from the brink of atrophy

I reach for the water bottle on my desk
to take pills to keep my heart on pace

I sigh

I am alive

And I have the world available to me as a beautiful promise

But...

It is all meaningless

~ d², 02.06.23, 11:59 PM

Ecclesiastes 2:4-9

4 I undertook great projects: I built houses for myself and planted vineyards. *5* I made gardens and parks and planted all kinds of fruit trees in them. *6* I made reservoirs to water groves of flourishing trees. *7* I bought male and female slaves and had other slaves who were born in my house. I also owned more herds and flocks than anyone in Jerusalem before me. *8* I amassed silver and gold for myself, and the treasure of kings and provinces. I acquired male and female singers, and a harem as well—the delights of a man's heart. *9* I became greater by far than anyone in Jerusalem before me. In all this my wisdom stayed with me.

Come Again?

Life happens by
choices of intention,
default, indifference,
or apathy

framed by how we view
our ability to wield control
or submit to edicts of happenstance

the minimum keeps balance
the maximum sparks progress
doing nothing hastens death

ambitious seeds exist in
contentment and complacency

the former feeds
a healthy spark
the latter starves it
in the dark

unwitting attachments to trauma
distort both the cheap seats
and the skybox view

consistent conflagrations of
mindful or mindless decisions
carefully or carelessly
craft out our realities

the devil lies in
calculated wait

within the details
of our ever-present
and ever-available
redemption is there
if we only
seek it and ask

~ d², 09.08.22, 11:25 PM

Ecclesiastes 2:4-9

Ecclesiastes 2:9-10

⁹ I became greater by far than anyone in Jerusalem before me. In all this my wisdom stayed with me.
¹⁰ I denied myself nothing my eyes desired;
 I refused my heart no pleasure.
My heart took delight in all my labor,
 and this was the reward for all my toil.

Mathematics

I function

to produce
a solution

I function

adding to
existing values

I function

subtracting
coveted vices

I function

dividing my energy
into infinite
fractions of costs

I function

multiplying fears
to an
exponential growth

I function

calculating and
crunching
situations into
monumental totals

Ecclesiastes 2:9-10

      I function

as a solvent
dimension erodes

      I function

angling for rights
triangulated
with the acute

      I function

basing binary
encoded purposes
undergirding
theorems proven
and disclosed
data dependent on
deficient
discovery
and
diametrically
dilated
to diagonal
digits
magnetically
opposed

      I function

Ecclesiastes 2:9-10

cosine(ing)
negative
arguments
distancing
components
balanced
equilaterally
setting up a
tidy sum

    I function

gradients of
gain
expanding codes
ratios
breathing
harmony

    I function

spinning on an
axis
anchored in
wisdom
cyclically piercing
ideal elements
imaginary and
complex
with an
impartial
improper
incidence

Ecclesiastes 2:9-10

    I function

circles
surrounding
an overloaded
matrix

    I function

jumping
hearts in
knots
level
and intertwine
into a lattice
and climb
limits on order

    I function

~ d^2, 10.12.16, 11:39 AM

Ecclesiastes 2:10-11

[10] I denied myself nothing my eyes desired;
　I refused my heart no pleasure.
My heart took delight in all my labor,
　and this was the reward for all my toil.
[11] Yet when I surveyed all that my hands had done
　and what I had toiled to achieve,
everything was meaningless, a chasing after the wind;
　nothing was gained under the sun.

Wisdom Invites Madness

Examine my heart
　　it beats
　　intricate melodies
　　intoxicating
　　on repeat

Examine my thoughts
　　inspiration
　　tracing genius
　　plotting against
　　defeat

Examine my hands
　　open for giving
　　gripped for living
　　raised for what
　　my religion holds

Examine my motives
　　pulls toward lofty goals
　　leading to darkness
　　buried with layers of
　　dirty folds

Examine my prayers
　　pleading and
　　praising
　　prying away from intercession
　　an unwarranted favor
　　seeking limitless grace

Examine my love
> balanced under the
> threshold of
> unconditional
> two steps behind
> the purest pace

Examine my feet
> scaling mountains
> climbing down stairs
> running empty races
> walking in despair

Examine my existence
> a philosophical
> conundrum
> questioning if I am really
> and truly
> here

~ d^2, 08.05.17, 11:21 AM

Ecclesiastes 2:10-11

Ecclesiastes 2:12-16

¹² Then I turned my thoughts to consider wisdom,
 and also madness and folly.
What more can the king's successor do
 than what has already been done?
¹³ I saw that wisdom is better than folly,
 just as light is better than darkness.
¹⁴ The wise have eyes in their heads,
 while the fool walks in the darkness;
but I came to realize
 that the same fate overtakes them both.
¹⁵ Then I said to myself,
 "The fate of the fool will overtake me also.
 What then do I gain by being wise?"
I said to myself,
 "This too is meaningless."
¹⁶ For the wise, like the fool, will not be long remembered;
 the days have already come when both have been forgotten.
Like the fool, the wise too must die!

An Incomplete Life

I love boxes
containers to store things
but mine are empty
they fill my shelves
after I collect from others'
heirlooms or garage sales
the more unique the better
they hold nothing

I love pretty packages
color coordinated with wrappings
bows and streamers
taped neatly on the folds
they are like pieces of art
ready to be ripped apart
but I always pause to marvel before doing so

I love finished puzzles
the angst at the start wanes
as I find complementing parts
searching for patterns and placement
and keeping on display, for days, once done

I love feel-good stories
a team conquers the game
heartbeats profess and accept love
a project has succeeded
a victory is won

These loves obscure
an understanding
that nothing is truly contained
nothing stays attractive
not all mysteries are solved
nothing is truly completed
this living is not the solution to life
it is a part of an infinite continuum

~ d², 09.19.22, 11:52 PM

Ecclesiastes 2:12-16

Ecclesiastes 2:12-16

On That Note
A response to Ecclesiastes 2:12-16

Crickets serenade me
at night
a combination of
free notes and
double-time crescendos
a frontline environmental improvisation
the half-diminished brother
to the hipster grasshopper
modulating along a
syncopated progression
swinging into an isolated solo
for a millisecond
striding along the full moon's timbre
confusing a well-timed vamp
for a structured verse
absent a human voice

~ d^2, 09.19.22, 11:26 PM

Anti-Matter

It doesn't matter
that my world is
chaotically crumbling
brick by brick tumbles
the foundation quickly
disintegrating and
rumbling into a powdery fog

It doesn't matter

It doesn't matter
that this body is
characteristically dying
aging to the date marked expiration
apathetic shifting of muscles
into adipose fat
riddled with aches antithetically
motivating stilted movement

It doesn't matter

It doesn't matter
that my mind slips to
graceless computing
synoptically missing
its clicks and snaps
fogs of emptiness
neglecting moments
exhausted cues to
lines long forgot

It doesn't matter

Ecclesiastes 2:17-23

[17] So I hated life, because the work that is done under the sun was grievous to me. All of it is meaningless, a chasing after the wind. [18] I hated all the things I had toiled for under the sun, because I must leave them to the one who comes after me. [19] And who knows whether that person will be wise or foolish? Yet they will have control over all the fruit of my toil into which I have poured my effort and skill under the sun. This too is meaningless. [20] So my heart began to despair over all my toilsome labor under the sun. [21] For a person may labor with wisdom, knowledge and skill, and then they must leave all they own to another who has not toiled for it. This too is meaningless and a great misfortune. [22] What do people get for all the toil and anxious striving with which they labor under the sun?

[23] All their days their work is grief and pain; even at night their minds do not rest. This too is meaningless.

Ecclesiastes 2:17-23

It doesn't matter
'cause
it is but a vapor
an illusion of reality
bereft of fulfillment and
eternal intent

It just doesn't matter

~ d², 06.06.15, 3:39 AM

Ambitious Wind

Top of the mark
number one in sales
elected class president
one destined to excel
reaping
ultimately the same fate
of number two, 20, or
one stuck in last place

earned degrees can't
prevent death, taxes, or disease
mortality is everyone's
consequence

The quest of Hughes[1]
was costly and trivial
making rich
five-star physicians
only to be conquered
by microbial
criminals

his remaining gains
became an unwitting
stranger's inheritance
creating generational
entitlement

---

[1] Howard Robert Hughes, Jr., Dec. 24, 1905-April 5, 1976.

Ecclesiastes 2:24-26

[24] *A person can do nothing better than to eat and drink and find satisfaction in their own toil. This too, I see, is from the hand of God,* [25] *for without him, who can eat or find enjoyment?* [26] *To the person who pleases him, God gives wisdom, knowledge and happiness, but to the sinner he gives the task of gathering and storing up wealth to hand it over to the one who pleases God. This too is meaningless, a chasing after the wind.*

Ecclesiastes 2:24-26

craving technology at its cheapest
with each version or
rebuild
its power increases

Does anyone REALLY know
how to operate
an abacus
or a slide rule?

Human hierarchy is a lie
obscuring an
appreciation of joy
immersed and ingrained
into the delicate
DNA
of every precious moment.

~ d^2, 08.05.17, 12:35 PM

The Book of Ecclesiastes, Chapter 3

She left an imprint. She walked on this earth and the dust will claim her. But her presence mattered and now we ache with the absence. But not even the waves crashing on the shore will erase the permanence of her love.

9.24.22, "Footprint in Sand, So Cliche"

Chain Gang

Everything is tethered
to the seconds on a clock
like a bomb
programmed to detonate
followed by ripples
aftershocks
initiated with pediatrician's
rear smacks
sparking lit filament
rapidly roaring conflagration
consuming
tightly woven fibers
inching toward
blast, transformative
pregnant possibilities
bursting at the seams
to maximum reach
and appropriate
exposure
multiple planetary
orbs of
Chronos
colliding
Big Banged Theologies
making insignificant appearances
deep within a fraction of
a singular
Kairos Moment

~ d², 08.05.17, 1:26 PM

Ecclesiastes 3:1-8

*¹There is a time for everything,
   and a season for every activity under the heavens:
² a time to be born and a time to die,
   a time to plant and a time to uproot,
³ a time to kill and a time to heal,
   a time to tear down and a time to build,
⁴ a time to weep and a time to laugh,
   a time to mourn and a time to dance,
⁵ a time to scatter stones and a time to gather them,
   a time to embrace and a time to refrain from embracing,
6 a time to search and a time to give up,
   a time to keep and a time to throw away,
⁷ a time to tear and a time to mend,
   a time to be silent and a time to speak,
⁸ a time to love and a time to hate,
   a time for war and a time for peace.*

Ecclesiastes 3:9-14

⁹ What do workers gain from their toil? ¹⁰ I have seen the burden God has laid on the human race. ¹¹ He has made everything beautiful in its time. He has also set eternity in the human heart; yet no one can fathom what God has done from beginning to end. ¹² I know that there is nothing better for people than to be happy and to do good while they live. ¹³ That each of them may eat and drink, and find satisfaction in all their toil—this is the gift of God. ¹⁴ I know that everything God does will endure forever; nothing can be added to it and nothing taken from it. God does it so that people will fear him.

What Is for You, Is for You

"God can present your blessing in a manner that not only moves others of out of your way, but moves you out of your way."—Notes from Bible Study

Divine appointment
aligning incongruent components
miraculously contorted
forming a blessed new
mowed out of competing interests
highlighting the improbable
doubting that nothing is too large for the Truth
who marvels at the formation
impermeable to counter influences
a structure orchestrated to follow
the melody of a heart's desire
tempered by
ordained paths
parting through a sea of naysayers
leaving room to
humbly march onward
leaving only
personal mountains
of embedded treachery
to comb through
begging to release
nits grabbing hold of roots

Are you willing to shave
yourself clean to
make it through?

~ d², 09.19.22, 6:34 PM

Third-Person Singular

It is
what it is
when it is
how it is

for the time
that it is

simultaneously
with all it is

purposed for that
which is

eternally propelled
as is

encompassing
everything
that is

honoring The One
that is

bringing back to
enmesh with what is

our past, present, future is

pale in comparison
with the larger
is

Ecclesiastes 3:15

15 Whatever is has already been, and what will be has been before; and God will call the past to account.

Ecclesiastes 3:15

twisting us
on our heads
to comply
is

the task
that is

insurmountable
for
it is

not our battle
but Hers/His

singularly

in triune
harmony

~ d², 01.31.23, 10:29 PM

The Newspaper, The Bible, and The Zoo

Environment controlled
bodies on view
are you deemed too violent?
or seeking hands to caress you?
custom-made ecosystems
sourced with the essentials to subdue
parading judgmental spectators
tossing cheap munchies to chew
caging potential and ambition
while broadcasting twisted truths
pampered privileged
choking on faked sly news
schedules of gilded exposure
are only granted to a few
once your sheen of popularity is worn
your carcass is a gutted stuffed statue
corporal beings rotating from
authority to oppression
as divinely assessed
déjà vu

~ d^2, 08.05.17, 3:26 PM

Ecclesiastes 3:16-22

[16] And I saw something else under the sun:
In the place of judgment—wickedness was there,
  in the place of justice—wickedness was there.
[17] I said to myself,
"God will bring into judgment
  both the righteous and the wicked,
for there will be a time for every activity,
  a time to judge every deed."
[18] I also said to myself, "As for humans, God tests them so that they may see that they are like the animals. [19] Surely the fate of human beings is like that of the animals; the same fate awaits them both: As one dies, so dies the other. All have the same breath[c]; humans have no advantage over animals. Everything is meaningless. [20] All go to the same place; all come from dust, and to dust all return. [21] Who knows if the human spirit rises upward and if the spirit of the animal goes down into the earth?"
[22] So I saw that there is nothing better for a person than to enjoy their work, because that is their lot. For who can bring them to see what will happen after them?

Ecclesiastes 3:16-22

Feeding Chaos

Scrolls of contrasting
opinions BREAKING
with self-import
restricted characters, and no more
unless notations of
threading philosophical insights exist
sub-tendered for extended points
reducing intelligent discourse to
highlight who has the loudest
voice
amplification begging for follows, hearts,
and quoted recycled parts
in agreement or
ridicule
comingling grief with
satire in just one swipe
attention spans are
reduced to tones
echoing in agreement, for
dissension is a threat
conquered by
reports, trolling, or the decision to ignore
honest debate is lost
we no longer want to
engage to grow
instead, we interact
to show
what we know
or to scale hierarchies and
clamber up ladders
propped on human footstools

Ecclesiastes 3:16-22

manipulated to appear
as mere
spotlights on the floor
granting zero introspection
a lure
of defensiveness
the only lauded and acceptable posture
battle lines drawn with
no possible points of compromise
it is surrender or retreat
we linger within intentional contrary measures
lobbying callous bombs of
pithy retorts and distorted images
for everything not symbiotic is
unwelcome clamor
defiantly positioned
black-and-white stalemates
disregarding the brilliant spectrums
of enlightening discourse which
open toward gradients of growth
or necessary evolutions of thought
all sides stay stuck blindly guarding their posts
oh how I yearn for the opportunity to truly
nuance the noise

~ d², 09.09.22, 11:55 PM

The Book of Ecclesiastes, Chapter 4

I stand on this shore seeking structure while overwhelmed. I need peace and the impossible, simultaneously. I look to stack stable blocks until I can see a pattern I can embrace, tunneling through undefined grief until I clearly see a goal. I am fighting with chaos and consequences, praying for a miracle to pass.

9.24.22, "It Just Rolls In"

Absence

The space between what is and what was
aches with a stench of emptiness never filled
we all walk with holes oozing out
memories linking to considerations
or ideologies that may not ever materialize
gaps that were often present before birth
a result of our arrival on earth

but we still breathe
pulling in air
that whistles
through the abandoned orifices
producing a tune
that can entertain
through its wanton melancholy

our heartbeats
create echoes bouncing through
chasms coated with
the struggle of hope versus apathy

healing is not a putty placed to cover or assuage

healing is a microscope digging into the
caverns life etches through our solid resolve to scream
that we are here

our blood flows through the remaining
intricate channels

bathing our souls in the energy to
cognitively conjure new realities

Ecclesiastes 4:1-4

⁴ Again I looked and saw all the oppression that was taking place under the sun:
I saw the tears of the oppressed—
*   and they have no comforter;*
power was on the side of their oppressors—
*   and they have no comforter.*
² And I declared that the dead,
*   who had already died,*
are happier than the living,
*   who are still alive.*
³ But better than both
*   is the one who has never been born,*
who has not seen the evil
*   that is done under the sun.*
⁴ And I saw that all toil and all achievement spring from one person's envy of another. This too is meaningless, a chasing after the wind.

Ecclesiastes 4:1-4

creating waves of undulating joy
ironically crashing into shores of
shared grief

leaving souvenirs in the sand to
collect, polish, and place on our shelves
to admire and one day

call us home

~ d², 01.17.23, 10:32 PM

Occupational Hazard

A string pulls
with pain through collapsed time
a refrain from
wiggling fingers to bring words
hovering to the physical plane
landing on obscure tarmacs to read
a resulting numbness
from missed attempts
marking the spot with searing dread
I shake off the stressful indulgences of
one last that could not wait
projects from pricks of inspiration
ignited like fireworks
without sound and empty sonic shakes
silent struggles to confront
needed rest versus needed activity
stillness beckons
yet entraps me
I break free to face enduring harsh judgments
self-indictments
swelling to close channels of life flowing
weakening my grip on insights
slipping from capture
I lapse into a void of regrets
I need to rest
but rest tortures me
taunts me with missed moments
threatening to escape my grasp
to trace this existence with paper and pen

~ d², 11.15.22, 11:44 PM

Ecclesiastes 4:5-7

*⁵ Fools fold their hands
and ruin themselves.
⁶ Better one handful with tranquility
than two handfuls with toil
and chasing after the wind.
⁷ Again I saw something meaningless
under the sun:*

Ecclesiastes 4:8

*8 There was a man all alone;
    he had neither son nor brother.
There was no end to his toil,
    yet his eyes were not content with his wealth.
"For whom am I toiling," he asked,
    "and why am I depriving myself of enjoyment?"
This too is meaningless—
    a miserable business!*

Head without Pillow

An aching solitude exists in both
power and tears
but within the last breath a community hears
the blessed community
our final escape
from parasitic silos
lingering while they ingest
die-off that bathes unborn cells
with toxic overwhelm
even the unconscious
fight for relevance
sitting down to eat
the vanquished with heartbeats
the irony...

The Victor
The Self-Centered
and The Fool

alike

chew on their own meat
filling their bellies
vainly attempting to nourish
and sustain
decimated
carcasses

~ d², 08.05.17, 4:25 PM

The Hive

Ecclesiastes 4:8

Tunnels & catacombs
built from sweat, grit, and waste
crafted into future
pre-gentrified real estate
burrowing highways
at a deadening pace
nervous activity
builds a future
race
climbing
underlying backs
leaving
traceable tracks
all to appease the waiting
hums of conformity
drowning out
opposing realities
programmed to binge
while
chasing cliff-hangered
finalities
carrots dangling
a pause at season's end
busy satisfying
one
equally flawed, but
still beheld amongst us
and yet
we can't take time to taste the honey

~ d², 08.05.17, 2:23 PM

Honoring The
LEGEND

FIRST BREATH: MAY 11, 1938
LAST SMILE: FEBRUARY 9, 2023

FOREVER IN OUR HEARTS & MEMORIES

FRANCES Jeanette BARCROFT DALTON

Frances Jeanette's Community

PRAYER OF FOCUS:
God, focus my mind, focus my words, focus my spirit as I humbly seek to honor you as I celebrate the gift you gave me in the life and rich legacy of Frances Jeanette Barcroft Dalton.

[READ ECCLESIASTES 4:9-12]

Please bear with me, this afternoon, as I share a very short message about

Frances Jeanette's Community.

[OPENING GREETINGS]

Good afternoon, everyone.

I just want to take a few moments to express my appreciation to those who helped usher Ramona and I toward this moment, this day.

To Her Church:
> We would like to wholeheartedly thank Trinity Episcopal Church: Cindy, in the office; John, the A/V coordinator; Faron, my momma's favorite choir director; Mrs. Berry, who helped pull all of the details for the reception together; various guilds and groups; and Reverend Jes Reeves for everything you have done to help us prepare for today. And I want to thank the entire congregation of this wonderful, historic church who embraced our family in 1983 when we moved to Pine Bluff for how much you loved my mother—thank you for being an integral part of her community.

Ecclesiastes 4:9-12

*⁹ Two are better than one,
  because they have a good return for their labor:
¹⁰ If either of them falls down,
  one can help the other up.
But pity anyone who falls
  and has no one to help them up.
¹¹ Also, if two lie down together, they will keep warm.
  But how can one keep warm alone?
¹² Though one may be overpowered,
  two can defend themselves.
A cord of three strands is not quickly broken.*

Ecclesiastes 4:9-12

To the City of Pine Bluff:
Thanks to this loving community of Pine Bluff for how you supported us through your cards, calls, visits, prayer, and words of comfort. Thank you for how you all made sure to always look after Ms. Fran as she made her way through the city, living her very vibrant life.

To Those Joining us on Facebook:
Thanks to those of you online, watching on Facebook. Both our family, and the friends that could not make it here in person, we appreciate your online presence. Thank you, her online community, for helping to keep her mind sharp, for providing great laughs, and for making her world richer while confined during COVID, her recovery from surgery, or when she just could not fall asleep at three o'clock at night.

To Our Beloved Sorority:
The comfort provided during today's Omega Omega service was so very moving. Thank you for the way you came out to show your love and support for our family. Thank you for loving on our Delta Dear and being true sisters to her over the years. In particular, I want to thank the Pine Bluff Alumnae Chapter and Delta Eta Chapter Sorors at the University of Pine Bluff.

To My Mother's Friends:
To all her other friends who don't fit into any of the other categories I mentioned before, thank you for prayers of strength and comfort and for your kind words of encouragement. And thank you for connecting with Ramona and I, sharing so many wonderful ways my

mother touched your life. Thank you for being a part of my mother's history. Thank you for being part of what made her the wonderful person she was.

To Our Friends:
Ramona and I have great friends. We both have amazing church families. There are not enough words to express what it means to have each and every one of you in our corners. And for those who have had the opportunity, thank you for allowing us to share our mother with you!

To Our Family:
To my amazing family, thank you for being family. Whether through blood or love.

To My Sister:
And special thanks from me to my beautiful sister—thank you for being you. Thank you for being that kind of great person who worked with me, over the years, to make sure we always pulled our creative forces together to love on and care for Momma with all the generosity and kindness we could muster and with all of the grace and passion she deserved.

Finally, thanks to God for gifting me, gifting all of us, with the opportunity to coexist at the same time that Frances Jeanette Barcroft Dalton graced this earthly place.

Community...

The power of community...

Ecclesiastes 4:9-12

Ecclesiastes 4:9-12

U-N-I-T-Y

Locked arms
withstand angry enemies

Chorales of courage
rise above dissenting calamity

Interceding feet
march past strong-held penitentiaries

Corporate prayers
glance collectively toward Divinity

But trust and see
all accomplished is mere vanity

For "Heaven on Earth" is found within
acts of community

~ d^2, 08.05.17, 5:24 PM

[PAUSE/BREATHE]

"Heaven on Earth" is found within acts of community...

[OPENING QUESTION]

What was is it like to grow up with a mother who, in my opinion—and if you see this memorial program, you know I mean—was larger than life?

Well, when that same woman has mastered the understanding that the more you love others, the more God equips you to love others even more...

And who also had a heart of gold.

And who also had a generous spirit.

And who also had a fervent thirst for a full and meaningful life.

And, in addition to all of that, had our wonderful daddy by her side.

What was all of that like?

It was fabulous

so, i became

>my mother
>sang to me
>as a baby
>so, i became a singer
>
>my father
>gave me a
>book of poetry
>so, i became a poet
>
>my mother
>taught me to be
>dramatic
>so, i became an actress

Ecclesiastes 4:9-12

Ecclesiastes 4:9-12

my father
stressed the
importance of math and science
so, i became an engineer

my mother
kissed and bandaged my finger
when i cut it
so, i became secure

my father
stood beside me
as i stood on my own
so, i became independent

my mother
dressed me
to make sure
i was warm
so, i became comforted

my father
scolded me
when i did something wrong
so, i became responsible

my mother
kissed me when
my heart was broke
so, i became compassionate

Ecclesiastes 4:9-12

my father
hugged me
for no reason at all
so, i became loved

my parents
loved me
each in their own way
and,
so, I became Me.

01.13.88

from the book *Becoming Aware*

(So we, my sister and I became, She and Me)

In the fleeting reality of life, the living of it, every station of it should be lived to its fullest, but your stored treasures have no eternal value, true value is found in

1. community,
2. your divine purpose, and
3. your ability to receive from and give to others the love of God.

God's overflowing love was lived out so graciously through her.

Through the beauty of her over-the-top expressions

And then, her community

Ecclesiastes 4:9-12

How community came together for her growing up.

How community came together for her in college.

How community came together for her through her Sorority.

How community came together for her through her marriage.

How community came to her through her travels.

How community came to her through my sister and I.

How community came to her through her God.

Each a beautiful point of how she, too, loved others through community

And also,

How she lived life on her own terms

But, yet she still never let go of God's Unchanging Hands

> *"Time is filled with swift transition,*
> *Naught of earth unmoved can stand,*
> *build your hopes on things eternal,*
> *Hold to God's unchanging hand"*[1]

---

[1] *"Hold to God's Unchanging Hands"* by Jennie Bain Wilson, (d. 3 September 1913) Public Domain

I have been reflecting on the opening lyrics of that song since she passed

[PAUSE/BREATHE]

In my sanctified imagination, I think of how God held Momma's and Daddy's hand while he transitioned

How God then, with Daddy at God's side held Momma's hand as she transitioned.

[PAUSE/BREATHE]

Y'all, this seems sudden—most of us had great plans, trips, projects, and ideas we were going to work out and enjoy with her.

This seems too soon. And unfair.

But, I know, we all know, my mother had a great life, and she lived every moment that she could to its fullest.

There are too many who leave this earth without ever experiencing a fraction of the fullness available to them on this planet.

And that is a shame and, quite honestly, a disservice to the gift of life that has been granted to each of us.

I beg each of you under the sound of my voice to make a commitment today to do the same as my momma…

Ecclesiastes 4:9-12

Ecclesiastes 4:9-12

Please join me in repeating this promise, inserting the moniker that describes your relationship with her:

"Frances, Frankie, Aunt Frankie, Momma, Fran, Mrs. Dalton, Momma D, Soror Dalton, and Glam-ma"

Momma,
I promise to live my life to the fullest.

Momma,
I promise to pour out the endless love that God has given to me serve and to bless others.

Momma,
I promise to never let go of God's unchanging hand.

In closing, please know that **WE KNOW** we are grieving.

There will be tears, wailing, gnashing of teeth, anger with God, and the slightest of regrets over missed opportunities to shower her with just a little bit more love… and that is natural, normal, and okay. God honors all of that.

We are hurting, we have a huge hole that will never be filled by another, but I trust that it will be filled with God's love for us.

So, for right now, I stand in the indescribable peace of The Lord and reflect on this point:

> *In 2003, Mommy, with God,
> held Daddy's hand.*
>
> *In 2023, God, with Daddy,
> held Mommy's hand.*

I hope you fully get this…

> *God, Jesus, and the Holy Spirit kept them both in their divine embraces as they both transitioned from this mortal land.*

I, also, rest my peace on the firm understanding that she,

Frances, Frankie, Aunt Frankie, Fran, Mrs. Dalton, Momma D, Soror Dalton, and Glam-ma

…Momma

built her hopes on things eternal.

She is now thoroughly understanding the full and complete joy of **"Holding on to God's Unchanging Hand"**

Ecclesiastes 4:9-12

Ecclesiastes 4:11

*11 Also, if two lie down together, they will keep warm.
But how can one keep warm alone?*

Secret Indiscretions

Feelings out of communication

Unable to portray them in poetry
    or prose

But there is a want

Years of accumulated
    emotions
must account for something

Not this ominous nothing that I am
    forced to compose

Still sorting out all of the
    significances –
afraid to admit that there are none

Need this catharsis so to move on

    Need to
        encapsulate what was felt
        wanted
        and needed in words

If trapped between the letters &
    symbols
then it can escape the looming
    presence in the universe of
    conscious thought

    I want to

Ecclesiastes 4:11

      use phrases that colorfully
          depict the passion
          the pleasure
          and the pain

Generate an idiom to satirize
    the anguish

Use paragraphs to clearly
    categorize the joy

A literary monument

A symphony so pleasing
    to hear
    that it creates
    a melancholy tear
        orchestrated by my
        thoughts to your ears

        ARE YOU
        LISTENING?

The dilemma rests in counter-intentions

    I wanted to...
        write about something else
        create love-filled sonnets
        and well-read odes

        Paint vibrant flowers
        and weave fabric of sensuous
                warmth

Ecclesiastes 4:11

        Create based on physical
        evidence

    Not imagined interludes

But that chance is lost—and that poem

Damn, it would have been great

I smile
now
at the missed possibilities

Its potential intensity causes me
        to sit in still wonder

        I wanted to shout it from
        the mountaintops in semaphore

Oh well,
guess it was meant for me   alone

Chaotic sensations surround
        each memory
Confusion pit
        against the discovery
            of a stable datum
                meant to produce order

Once the smoke clears
        what bodies will be found to lie
        in the debris?

Ecclesiastes 4:11

Morbid curiosity compels me to
peer through the dissipating smoke
to see...

Will there be surprise at what is
discovered?

Secret Indiscretions–being slowly
disclosed

Quiet irregularities
    harmonies out of sync
Clouds, dark and discolored
    haphazard motions
     orange passions
     red grief
Syncopated dial tones
Scratches on a CD
    white sorrow
     green heat
Bitter Joy
Precious defeat
Compassionate abuse
    fuchsia disappointment
A lover's sweet retreat
    hungry chapped lips
Dreaded excitement
    "fiend-ing" for pain
Callous promises
      Angel seduction
    lime depression

Ecclesiastes 4:11

Lipstick on teeth
           sandpaper caressed cheeks
Inconsistent melodies
           estranged engagements

Two left feet.

~ d^2, 03.06.00, 5:20 PM
Long Beach California Airport

Cycles

History
repeats
and eats its own
tail
if not fed
a new
diet of
hope
and redemption

~ d², 06.05.22, 9:12 AM

Ecclesiastes 4:13-16

¹³ Better a poor but wise youth than an old but foolish king who no longer knows how to heed a warning. ¹⁴ The youth may have come from prison to the kingship, or he may have been born in poverty within his kingdom.
¹⁵ I saw that all who lived and walked under the sun followed the youth, the king's successor. ¹⁶ There was no end to all the people who were before them. But those who came later were not pleased with the successor. This too is meaningless, a chasing after the wind.

The Book of Ecclesiastes, Chapter 5

Let the Church Say Amen

It was EARLY when the palm hit my thigh

And I was willing, and the creek didn't rise

We celebrated God's goodness of any
    and all time

Coming not when we wanted,
    but always on time

Giving all honor, as we take our time

Turning to our neighbor, with doors open wide

Closing with joy, surpassing all understanding
    and time

Ecclesiastes 5:1

⁵ Guard your steps when you go to the house of God. Go near to listen rather than to offer the sacrifice of fools, who do not know that they do wrong.

Ecclesiastes 5:2

[2] *Do not be quick with your mouth,*
  do not be hasty in your heart
  to utter anything before God.
God is in heaven
  and you are on earth,
  so let your words be few.

What Do I Know?

My eyes
grab
a hold of objects in view
to inspect as I uncover

my awareness is shaped by that

the lens is limited to a
manipulation of focus
dependent on whether or not
the glass has been properly cleaned

using a dust-free cloth to scatter lint
hell-bent
on distorting the image

or

oil residue on the skin
rubbed marks
as evidence

my unique prints
of my obtuse ego
are a laden influence

what is captured in the raw
must be refined in post

and post is where the heart
forms the footage into a story
that others want to see

to be entertained
or informed

color-coded events to match
a desired palette
scrubbing voices to tone up a tune
that wants to be heard

I sit in my chair seeking to create
my definition of perfection.

altering time to sync up my predetermined beats
an orchestration of my singular purpose

a purpose sitting, on a remote island, far away

a caste away from others

floating in an ocean, a mere speck of existence in the vast body of God

I am under the impression that I am creating a seismic shift for humanity

in reality, I am barely generating a ripple effect in The Creator's wake.

~ d², 10.24.23, 11:45 AM

Ecclesiastes 5:2

Ecclesiastes 5:3

[3] A dream comes when there are many cares,
  and many words mark the speech of a fool.

D.N.R.

there is a dampness
attached to stale dreams
primed to erode
disintegrate
rust out
die
until becoming
invisible
memories

residue of
grieved hope
seeking to
resuscitate
defibrillate
revive
dysfunctional
conception
lacking power to
take root

~ d^2, 06.23.19, 12:24 AM

Make Haste

Dreams are like
cut flowers
ideas drastically severed
from their healthy
roots
smelling pretty and
artificially sustained
through a mixture of
water and the florist's
prepackaged additives

    the packet we usually throw away

until they ultimately
wilt and shrivel

unless, instead

we take a vibrant
clipping
soaked to nurture
and develop its own roots

detaching from its parent
requires swift action
or else you have just
simply pruned...

...waste...

...wasting the potential of a vibrant life
to our laziness

Ecclesiastes 5:4-7

[4] When you make a vow to God, do not delay to fulfill it. He has no pleasure in fools; fulfill your vow. [5] It is better not to make a vow than to make one and not fulfill it. [6] Do not let your mouth lead you into sin. And do not protest to the temple messenger, "My vow was a mistake." Why should God be angry at what you say and destroy the work of your hands? [7] Much dreaming and many words are meaningless. Therefore fear God.

Ecclesiastes 5:4-7

squandering an opportunity to foster a
resurgence of life

the orphaned branch finds
our confessions of neglect
useless, as it predictably
withers and dies.

~ d², 10.24.23, 11:59 AM

Tending Co-Dependently

I prune grapes
struggling to survive
allowing branches to thrive
with lighter loads
packing moth-gnawed satchels
with fruit bursting of
spoiled promises and
underdeveloped hope
empty of sustenance
hypnotically trapped by
the wafting poison of putrefaction
rotting orbs of weighted decay
tugging on fraying straps
pinching, digging raw trenches
tender channels through muscles fatigued
framing shoulders slumped
curving spines to counterbalance
in destructive symmetry
while strolling through
vineyards deeded to
unwelcoming others
callously trespassing
with no base to unload

~ d^2, 12.13.22

Ecclesiastes 5:8-9

[8] *If you see the poor oppressed in a district, and justice and rights denied, do not be surprised at such things; for one official is eyed by a higher one, and over them both are others higher still.* [9] *The increase from the land is taken by all; the king himself profits from the fields.*

Ecclesiastes 5:10-12

[10] *Whoever loves money never has enough;*
  whoever loves wealth is never satisfied with their income.
    This too is meaningless.
[11] *As goods increase,*
  so do those who consume them.
And what benefit are they to the owners
  except to feast their eyes on them?
[12] *The sleep of a laborer is sweet,*
  whether they eat little or much,
but as for the rich, their abundance
  permits them no sleep.

Yearnings

Thoughts stretched beyond
boundaries of appropriate measures
overlapping loose lids
of too-small containers
oozing over edges
solidifying before pooling
    onto the counter or floor
congealed paths lead to its dreaded halt
empty and fruitless conclusions
bubbles tapering to naught
dangling monuments of
unfulfilled passions
left lingering dry and tacky
to the touch
coated with the residue of
unrequited lusts
shrugged off as
par for the course
at this age and station
because
control is canon
alone
solemn
barren
but resolutely
a must

~ d², 09.07.22, 11:45 PM

Compartment Store

Pocketed, shuttered,
separated but aligned
with matching similarities

agreements of rogue considerations
arbitrary points of familiar
once confirmed seem
normal and expected

anticipating
intents of finding
purposes of each gathering

a home
sweet home
beautifully staged for
prospective views

or appointed with
color-coordinated
archived monuments

birthed from sourced recycled goods
negating the need to
risk a purchase anew

voiding transactions
purging clutter
repurpose, reuse
even if weathered, worn, torn

Ecclesiastes 5:13-16a

[13] *I have seen a grievous evil under the sun:*
wealth hoarded to the harm of its owners,
[14] *   or wealth lost through some misfortune,*
so that when they have children
*   there is nothing left for them to inherit.*
[15] *Everyone comes naked from their mother's womb,*
*   and as everyone comes, so they depart.*
They take nothing from their toil
*   that they can carry in their hands.*
[16] *This too is a grievous evil:*

Ecclesiastes 5:13-16a

yesterday's contraband

smuggled...

...imported
...infiltrated
...infected

though polluting future present treasured truths

~ d², 09.07.22, 11:45 PM

Joy, Now!

a toy box
full
before we crawled
to exploit
proclaiming "Mine"
when another gets
coveting the one
not grabbed yet
ignoring what is held
plotting to call "NEXT"
anxious with measure
increase to pleasure
this abundance comes with
grander
responsibilities
both the idiot and miser
are consumed with greed
both with a sales pitch
to over-promise or mislead
thus, the curse of those who
delight in
transforming wants
into
needs

~ d², 08.05.17, 6:53 PM

Ecclesiastes 5:16b-20

As everyone comes, so they depart,
 and what do they gain,
 since they toil for the wind?
[17] All their days they eat in darkness,
 with great frustration, affliction and anger.
[18] This is what I have observed to be good: that it is appropriate for a person to eat, to drink and to find satisfaction in their toilsome labor under the sun during the few days of life God has given them—for this is their lot. [19] Moreover, when God gives someone wealth and possessions, and the ability to enjoy them, to accept their lot and be happy in their toil—this is a gift of God. [20] They seldom reflect on the days of their life, because God keeps them occupied with gladness of heart.

The Book of Ecclesiastes, Chapter 6

We seek freedom from oppression like cracking the yolk from an egg, or waves of foam bubbles bursting on the sharp, jagged edges of rocks, confusing the concept of the trauma response of seeking freedom FROM others with the communal liberation within the fight for freedom FOR others.

9.24.22, "They Are Covered"

I Have No Heirs

My bloodline ends
with me

and I tried
at least six times

my body
and my choices
failed me

I tried

I possess a treasure trove
of family memories
and insights with
no progeny
to grab a hold of a
genetic legacy

only loose connections
gathered from
a discarded relationship
which I am at
their mercy to uphold

but I still want to pass
my historic gold

my heart overflows with
the jewels of tribal love
passed down through
dysfunctional struggles

Ecclesiastes 6:1-2

⁶ I have seen another evil under the sun, and it weighs heavily on mankind: ² God gives some people wealth, possessions and honor, so that they lack nothing their hearts desire, but God does not grant them the ability to enjoy them, and strangers enjoy
them instead.
This is meaningless, a grievous evil.

Ecclesiastes 6:1-2

I so easily could not
be

but they held on for me

but, I had no grasp
to pass
these precious mementos of a
glorious past

I stack trunks of photos
filled with smiles and features
that no one else can claim
generational ownership

I want to pass on their impact
to someone who gets it
and gets to share it
at least one generation more

but, I have no succession plan
in my blood line

so strangers
who come to cart away
my treasures
will get the rights to assign and ascribe
their intrinsic and implied value

They get to define
what will be their
future joy

Oh, God, the indescribable
ache of letting go

the hope of genetic legacy
lapses

a future paid for with sacrifices
that died in my parents' eyes

and I
lament that the
memories, moments, meditations, and mores
are dying with me

and yet...

It is meaningless

and it sucks.

~ d2, 10.25.23, 11:57 PM

Ecclesiastes 6:1-2

Ecclesiastes 6:3-6

³ A man may have a hundred children and live many years; yet no matter how long he lives, if he cannot enjoy his prosperity and does not receive proper burial, I say that a stillborn child is better off than he. ⁴ It comes without meaning, it departs in darkness, and in darkness its name is shrouded. ⁵ Though it never saw the sun or knew anything, it has more rest than does that man—
⁶ even if he lives a thousand years twice over but fails to enjoy his prosperity. Do not all go to the same place?

Do You

Do you...

know the treasure
in the brushed satin and spring of your skin
recoiling anew
unaware of decay and destruction
as a function of time?

Please savor it.

Do you...

feel your blood smoothly
racing through
unrestricted by calcification
feeding thoughts
motivated by naive grandeur
unmarred by disappointments?

Soak in it.

Do you...

write them down in journals
absent of lines
constraining to rules
you choose not to follow
with space to twist considerations into
lyrics laced with 20/20 sight?

Flow with it.

Ecclesiastes 6:3-6

Do you...

target a perception of utopia
the elders carelessly missed with
new songs lifted to beats of drums
coaxed through by hands furiously pounding
before the era of skin folds and callouses?

Sway to it.

Do you...

hold on to the vibrancy of life
filling your ample and agile lungs
exhaling a wonder
untainted by unfulfilled hopes
now entombed?

Breathe in it and—

Do you.

~ d^2, 09.27.22, 10:27 PM

Ecclesiastes 6:7-12

[7] *Everyone's toil is for their mouth,
   yet their appetite is never satisfied.*
[8] *What advantage have the wise over fools?
What do the poor gain
   by knowing how to conduct themselves before others?*
[9] *Better what the eye sees
   than the roving of the appetite.
This too is meaningless,
   a chasing after the wind.*
[10] *Whatever exists has already been named,
   and what humanity is has been known;
no one can contend
   with someone who is stronger.*
[11] *The more the words,
   the less the meaning,
   and how does that profit anyone?*
[12] *For who knows what is good for a person in life, during the few and meaningless days they pass through like a shadow? Who can tell them what will happen under the sun after they are gone?*

Chasing the Wind

I dreamt it

I designed it

I saw it

I smelled it

I touched it

I liked it

I coveted it

I wanted it

I yearned for it

I ached for it

I plotted for it

I sacrificed for it

I lied for it

Now, I need it

So, I'm entitled to it

"MINE!"

~ d², 08.05.17, 7:27 PM

The Book of Ecclesiastes, Chapter 7

Desiring connection at the cost of treasured fragments, birthed in the hopes gestated from a mother's womb, now replaced with remnants... You settled for loose threads of attachment, knitting a garment of community that does not suit you but fractures, leaving a heart in pieces.

9.24.22, "Impact"

Scavengers

You abused a corpse—necrophilia
excavating the wounds of your soil
snatched and piled for prostitution
by those who brokered your soul

Find divinity in everything
without corrupting The Divine

What if we loved on our trauma
celebrated what we
label perverse and profane

The ethos of "Ephesians" bathed in the spirit of "Acts"
and "1 John"

   —toward one body, reconciled and whole
   —toward one call, inspired and followed
   —toward one fellowship, pure and complete

*not necessarily calling for a direct quote,
but for a pattern of exploration*

Then, after you heal
you can freely traverse through
the stages of grief & radical discovery

~ d², 09.20.22, 10:34 PM

Ecclesiastes 7:1-5

⁷ A good name is better than fine perfume,
   and the day of death better than the day of birth.
² It is better to go to a house of mourning
   than to go to a house of feasting,
for death is the destiny of everyone;
   the living should take this to heart.
³ Frustration is better than laughter,
   because a sad face is good for the heart.
⁴ The heart of the wise is in the house of mourning,
   but the heart of fools is in the house of pleasure.
⁵ It is better to heed the rebuke of a wise person
   than to listen to the song of fools.

Ecclesiastes 7:6

6 Like the crackling of thorns under the pot,
　so is the laughter of fools.
　This too is meaningless.

White Noise

I seek to complete
a task that
is totally unique

and the steps
out of context seem
nebulous

and unwelcome

sightseers peek into
my cracks
and insert opinions
and unsolicited critique

pulling me to paralysis
or subjective apathy

I have a feat
that I seek
birthed in my heart by my
peace

so I must adjust my receipt of this noise
into productive focusing
chatter

~ d^2, 10.24.23, 12:05 PM

Punch & Judy

Pillars, established
with lofty ideals

built on threads
of unresolved shame

unhealed terror of
public exposure and
cataclysmic collapse

they scramble to fight
against
marionettes' manipulation

their puppeteer

twisting the cyclone of panic
to fight being revealed

until

the strength is gathered to
expose the game

and cut the strings

~ d², 10.24.23, 12:11 PM

Ecclesiastes 7:7a

7a Extortion turns a wise person into a fool,

Ecclesiastes 7:7b

7b *and a bribe corrupts the heart.*

Sticker Shock

All things being equal
is an illusion

the unattainable axiom of
the concept of fair fights

the banal falsehoods
of producing pure outcomes
to celebrate unfettered success
to lay the weak foundation
of lessons for evolution

Easy ways outs
cripple both the
affirming joy of the
human condition
and
our moral need to
develop and grow

winning at any cost
costs more than the physical tender
used in its exchange.

~ d², 10.24.23, 2:09 PM

The End of the Matter

As we chase goals

targets

results

we lose sight of
the ability to be
in everything
every moment and thus
we hinge our joy on
to-do lists
checked

line items crossed off

the ability to
sit at the end
and reflect in peace
and comfort
in the calm
after the storm

in those terms

within those
parameters
it is better

and that
better is a social construct focused
on keeping us on a

Ecclesiastes 7:8a

8a *The end of a matter is better than its beginning,*

Ecclesiastes 7:8a

mindless
rotating
wheel

hamsters chasing the next accomplishment

and it is a meaningless pursuit

but one that still
produces a high

the rush of positive
endorphins attached to
marking something
done

but it does not belie or diminish the ultimate

it is written
and it is done

toil is meaningless

results are meaningless

but to arrive at the ultimate end,
there is perfected joy

~ d², 10.26.23, 11:15 PM

Ego Trap

When I neglect
to wait on God
my arrogance pushes me
to GET my wants
camouflaged as needs met
    as a function of the grandeur of me
and I miss out on
experiencing the
wonders in the untraceable
movements of
God

~ d², 10.26.23, 11:27 PM

Ecclesiastes 7:8b

⁸ᵇ *and patience is better than pride.*

Ecclesiastes 7:9

⁹ *Do not be quickly provoked in your spirit,*
  for anger resides in the lap of fools.

Tender-Hearted

He who holds my
heart
will determine
the pressure of the grasp
whether it is cradled with care
to allow the
echoes of life
to bounce as designed
or mindlessly
gripped
with absent-minded force
strangling out
good judgment

accelerating flows
to empty chambers
inverted into
vacuums
hastily sucking
back in supply

forcing measures to
increase the beat
to meet
and rapidly stabilize the flow

~ d², 10.30.23, 11:50 PM

Hindsight Is Not 20/20

What a gift it is
to look back
with fondness

editing out harsh edges
that are incompatible
with frames bought to store them

they are romantic reflections
cherished memories
aired out to
remove the stench
of shame or regret

and yet

existing in spent
timelines unfit to measure
and chastising the linear development
of now

the wisdom gained
in archives acts out

glossing over the
scars, incremental steps
to our current elevation

our best is yet to come
it is not the selective recall of our
rose-colored filtered past.

~ d², 10.31.23, 12:02 AM

Ecclesiastes 7:10

[10] Do not say, "Why were the old days better than these?"
  For it is not wise to ask such questions.

Ecclesiastes 7:11-12

[11] Wisdom, like an inheritance, is a good thing
  and benefits those who see the sun.
[12] Wisdom is a shelter
  as money is a shelter,
but the advantage of knowledge is this:
  Wisdom preserves those who have it.

The Survival Game

At conception
beating million to one odds
to produce a living vessel

During gestation
we are surrounded by
instruments for our survival

Nothing more—nothing less

A perfect balance
to produce a perfect birth

Any introduction of
irrelevant matter
tilts the scales toward non-optimal results

At birth
our spiritually integrated development ensues

> From can't breathe to grasping the first breath
> From can't see to raising the eyelids
> From can't rise up to movement at will
> From can't roll to rolling
> From can't crawl to crawling
> From can't walk to walking

The progression from can't brought about from
overcoming obstacles of equal magnitude

The greater the odds, the greater the rewards

So, we develop only from what we overcome

We overcome so we can develop

> and we develop so we can play a game
> and we play a game to reach a goal
> and as we reach our goal, we make a move

closer to or further from our survival

With genetically ingrained instructions
naturally we choose to succumb

We chose this out of irresponsibility

We chose this so we can have a game
but we forget that it was our choice

so we must go from

> Can't perceive to aware
> Can't comprehend to understand
> Can't know to total knowing-ness

Doing this on every playing field
until this crazy game is over

and all of its insane players have won

~ d², 09.18.00

Ecclesiastes 7:11-12

Ecclesiastes 7:13-14

¹³ Consider what God has done:
Who can straighten
 what he has made crooked?
¹⁴ When times are good, be happy;
 but when times are bad, consider this:
God has made the one
 as well as the other.
Therefore, no one can discover
 anything about their future.

Balance

He cried
we connected

She laughed
we deflected

Compassion
draws in others

Happiness
exists on its own

Joy
is the evidence of both

The proof of God's reward

I failed
came back resilient

I succeeded
I grew indignant

Breakthroughs
build strength and character

Triumph
is its own reward

Wisdom considers these as parallel companions
Where The Fool promptly ignores

~ d^2, 08.05.17, 8:42 PM

Meaning & Purpose

In life there is purpose
in living there is meaninglessness
in the now there is the opportunity
to embrace the joy of it all

contentment

even in the most purpose-filled life,
the daily machinations are meaningless
and contentment is a prize
waiting to be uncovered and found

though, instead of searching
learn to relish sitting in it

the meaninglessness

for

If all things have purpose
and all actions are meaningless
we ease into a glorious place of contentment
without sinking into the hopelessness

the sour breath of complacency

for meaninglessness does not beget hopelessness, the futile and fatal tool that births the apathy of it all

complacency rejects purpose of any kind

complacency depends on a meaning

Ecclesiastes 7:15-23

[15] In this meaningless life of mine I have seen both of these:
the righteous perishing in their righteousness,
    and the wicked living long in their wickedness.
[16] Do not be overrighteous,
    neither be overwise—
    why destroy yourself?
[17] Do not be overwicked,
    and do not be a fool—
    why die before your time?
[18] It is good to grasp the one
    and not let go of the other.
    Whoever fears God will avoid all extremes.
[19] Wisdom makes one wise person more powerful
    than ten rulers in a city.
[20] Indeed, there is no one on earth who is righteous,
    no one who does what is right and never sins.
[21] Do not pay attention to every word people say,
    or you may hear your servant cursing you—
[22] for you know in your heart
    that many times you yourself have cursed others.

[23] All this I tested by wisdom and I said,

"I am determined to be wise"—
    but this was beyond me.

Ecclesiastes 7:15-23

to extract its hopelessness from
so, meaning is as useless as it is hopeless

the only value in life is purpose

aligning to purpose,
orders our choices,
prepares our sacrifices,
structures our priorities

in perfect meaningless fashion

embrace meaninglessness
it is the prime leveler

balancing every equation
toward the same one

under the sun, because of the Son

meaning is pointless, purpose is not

purpose assigns our power to the entity
greater than ourselves and that will serve eternity

brilliantly

~ d², 09.27.22, 10:27 PM

I Bleed

Content Warning: Imagery of Cutting

I slice open my tender
exposed skin revealing
through razor
thin lines hesitantly encouraged
pools of dark red epiphanies

to gather

oozing insights,
overwhelming complexities
of dripping
unavoidable
human
stains

oxidizing out regrettable spots to
prove that I am living

I am alive

but the drips
coagulate to hinder fatal consequences

wounded

wounds healed are often sliced anew
exposing hastily, ill-informed restructuring
laying bare resulting cultural keloids
puffed-up masses

over unacknowledged unexplored traumas

Ecclesiastes 7:13-27

[23]"I am determined to be wise"—
   but this was beyond me.
[24] Whatever exists is far off and most profound—
   who can discover it?
[25] So I turned my mind to understand,
   to investigate and to search out
wisdom and the scheme of things
and to understand the stupidity of wickedness
   and the madness of folly.
[26] I find more bitter than death
   the woman who is a snare,
whose heart is a trap
   and whose hands are chains.
The man who pleases God will escape her,
   but the sinner she will ensnare.
[27] "Look," says the Teacher, "this is what I have discovered:

Ecclesiastes 7:23-27

generational
sociological
psychological

all are attacked
surgically
skillfully
with searing precision

puncturing taunt bubbles laying bare and

philosophically

examining,

approaching cautious retuning and now,

again my

scars are ripped open,

stripper fan dance revealing
raw vulnerable flesh

down to the white meat

whimpering and begging
for the harsh sting of antiseptic sermons

prophetic points of pontification
scraping free calcified deposits

of sins and lies

and

I bleed, often,
to prove that I possess life

~ d², 11.20.22, 11:00 PM

Ecclesiastes 7:23-27

Ecclesiastes 7:23-29

"Adding one thing to another to discover the scheme of things—
[28] while I was still searching but not finding—
I found one upright man among a thousand,
but not one upright woman among them all.
[29] This only have I found:
God created mankind upright,
but they have gone in search of many schemes."

Rodents and Mazes

Begin with the end in mind
now obscure it
devise multiple schemes
to get to it
layer with traps to delay
moving through it
present the mystery to others
to travel to it
temper your wise counsel
'cause you foreknew it
grant mercy with hints
allow them to view it
celebrate their victory
you want them to do it
now mentor their path
so they can redo it
begin with the end in mind
now obscure it

~ d², 08.05.17, 9:25 PM

The Book of Ecclesiastes, Chapter 8

I want to replace negativity and grief with platitudes of joy and peace. I want to twist my self-doubt and regret into empowerment. I am seeking ways to translate itinerant programming from failures to launch to boards of success, but I digress, only to remind myself, in all things, to always strive toward my best.

9.24.22, "Solitude"

Fine Craftsmanship

>Knowledge cuts
>through ignorance
>
>Wisdom cushions
>the blow
>
>Knowledge renders
>sharp judgment
>
>Wisdom corrects
>to grow
>
>Knowledge is captured
>from books and the Internet
>
>Wisdom is obtained
>through compassion and trials
>
>The knowledgeable find joy
>in facts and figures
>
>The wise find joy
>in living Life

~ d², 08.05.17, 10:25 PM

Ecclesiastes 8:1

¹Who is like the wise?
Who knows the explanation of things?
A person's wisdom brightens their face
and changes its hard appearance.

Ecclesiastes 8:2-9

² Obey the king's command, I say, because you took an oath before God.
³ Do not be in a hurry to leave the king's presence. Do not stand up for a bad cause, for he will do whatever he pleases.
⁴ Since a king's word is supreme, who can say to him, "What are you doing?"
⁵ Whoever obeys his command will come to no harm,
 and the wise heart will know the proper time and procedure.
⁶ For there is a proper time and procedure for every matter,
 though a person may be weighed down by misery.
⁷ Since no one knows the future,
 who can tell someone else what is to come?
⁸ As no one has power over the wind to contain it,
 so[a] no one has power over the time of their death.
As no one is discharged in time of war,
 so wickedness will not release those who practice it.
⁹ All this I saw, as I applied my mind to everything done under the sun. There is a time when a man lords it over others to his own hurt.

Free to Move About the Cabin

I grew up in
an era when
plane crashes
were deemed inevitable
almost seen as a casual annual

the errors of the
past have birthed
numerous delays
of treasured safety

so grateful for advancements

I SMDH at those who
seek, through malice,
to lessen our odds

why would they take the option
to gamble

it is the snake eating its own tail
choking on its venomous evil

but, even the most skilled
can't predict mechanical or
environmental calamity

~ d², 10.31.23, 1:43 AM

Up on the Rooftop

The action started from
My bones
> that shook
> excited my cells and caused
> them to vibrate and each
> movement radiated outward
> until my skin ignited with
> a sensuous warmth

Then I felt alive
> > 'Up on the rooftop'

My vision
> stimulated from
> my corneal copulation
> with the universe
> caused my sight to
> expand beyond its reach—

I saw things wonderful
> > 'Up on the rooftop'

Then the breeze
> timed with a Swiss
> clock's precision
> stirred around over
> and through me
> sensually cooling me off
> during the humidity of my
> burdens
> and the heat of my passions

I got caught up in a whirlpool of
> movement
> > 'Up on the rooftop'

~ d², 1999

Ecclesiastes 8:8

⁸ As no one has power over the wind to contain it,
  so[a] no one has power over the time of their death.
As no one is discharged in time of war,
  so wickedness will not release those who practice it.

Ecclesiastes 8:10-13

[10] Then too, I saw the wicked buried—those who used to come and go from the holy place and receive praise[c] in the city where they did this. This too is meaningless.
[11] When the sentence for a crime is not quickly carried out, people's hearts are filled with schemes to do wrong. [12] Although a wicked person who commits a hundred crimes may live a long time, I know that it will go better with those who fear God, who are reverent before him. [13] Yet because the wicked do not fear God, it will not go well with them, and their days will not lengthen like a shadow.

Dead Things
ref. Matthew 8:22

Stored bodies crumpled
in haphazard piles
exhibiting
varying levels
of decay
rotting, putrefying
baking a feast for the
larvae hatched from eggs
developing the wing-spawned pupae,
ready to flutter away...
...to a new space

A graven stench
permeates the atmosphere
imprisoning the living
behind its foul bars
providing perverse
comfort and peace

Home Sweet Home
to the wretched and
the unreleased
furnished from
vast catalogs of issues
eternally bouncing
on a grief-staged
parade
   mail-order
   store-bought
   and even some pieces
   custom-made

Ecclesiastes 8:10-13

Denying the forgotten
ironic connections
while still craving the
desire to move
far, far away from

An identity
hope
happiness manufactured
a catalyst for memorable moments
nurturing life and living
controlled by an
uneducated
unspiritual
desperate
yearning for
a better day

Tagged for ownership
but bankrupt and
unable to afford
the price to pay
dysfunctional
exhibitions of
responsibility
stunting
well-meaning
gestures
of care

Ecclesiastes 8:10-13

Empty boxes
strewn without compassion
symbols of overwhelm

Stress personified: felt, tasted, and worn

Ignoring the
salvific beckoning
to walk away
and nix the mourning
so to

Let the dead
bury the dead

~ d², 04.21.14, 7:17 PM

No Way Out

Stressing over
which bill to pay next
just got word
paycheck is less
economic tunnel vision
ushers in a global subclass
cast eyes down from luxury
settle for the beauty in trash

cancel the gaze upon product placement
in movies and on TV
refuse the programmed
futile fantasy
cherish simple pleasures
though society flaunts
complex needs
two steps toward advancement
viewed by the opulent
appears as groveling on your knees
must follow the law to the letter
where Affluenza gets a hand slap
and a lecture to do better
where bankruptcy from
a billionaire is shrewd
if a pauper
means you're screwed

but

Ecclesiastes 8:14-17

[14] There is something else meaningless that occurs on earth: the righteous who get what the wicked deserve, and the wicked who get what the righteous deserve. This too, I say, is meaningless. [15] So I commend the enjoyment of life, because there is nothing better for a person under the sun than to eat and drink and be glad. Then joy will accompany them in their toil all the days of the life God has given them under the sun.
[16] When I applied my mind to know wisdom and to observe the labor that is done on earth—people getting no sleep day or night— [17] then I saw all that God has done. No one can comprehend what goes on under the sun. Despite all their efforts to search it out, no one can discover its meaning. Even if the wise claim they know, they cannot really comprehend it.

Ecclesiastes 8:14-17

simple is the uncluttered joy
found in this humble place
the wealthy can afford a shovel
to uncover it from the layer of baubles

but

just in case
they'll still worship their valuables

~ d², 08.05.17, 11:44 PM

The Book of Ecclesiastes, Chapter 9

I need time to be without the attachments that define my purpose, position, or relations. I want to not be daughter, caregiver, sister, friend, mother, grandmother, lover, bed warmer, the compassionate listening ear. I want to exist between the lines of purpose and destiny, floating in the ennui of it all, relishing the ability to exist in an oblivious, total fullness, without having to achieve "a this" or "a that." I just want to soak up a few cocktails and chill.

9.24.22, "Pier Issues"

Cracked Mirror

A reflection
jaded
by a careless break

distortions based on angles
of misplacement
showing multifaceted
prisms of likenesses
comical and favorable at once

remnants, shards gather
in inconspicuous corners
catching flesh unguarded
to bleed out
our reckoning
with mortality

humanity
what makes us real
pushing us beyond
artificial visages

prompting deeper inspections of
our souls
our character
our world

reducing them to convenient
references

a mere disposable tool
at our disposal

Ecclesiastes 9:1-2a

⁹ So I reflected on all this and concluded that the righteous and the wise and what they do are in God's hands, but no one knows whether love or hate awaits them. ² All share a common destiny—the righteous and the wicked, the good and the bad, the clean and the unclean, those who offer sacrifices and those who do not.

Ecclesiastes 9:1-2a

not a hard and fast rule
it is what it is
a mere image
a reflection
not our gospel

~ d², 06.26.21, 12:19 PM

Pushing It

The child who teeters
too close to the edge

The assignment submitted
with one second left

Your mother's 911 message
left on unread

The phone 2%
from going dead

The lover quickly
leaving your bed

~ d², 06.27.21, 5:26 AM

Ecclesiastes 9:2b-4

As it is with the good,
   so with the sinful;
as it is with those who take oaths,
   so with those who are afraid to take them.
³ This is the evil in everything that happens under the sun: The same destiny overtakes all. The hearts of people, moreover, are full of evil and there is madness in their hearts while they live, and afterward they join the dead.
⁴ Anyone who is among the living has hope—even a live dog is better off than a dead lion!

Ecclesiastes 9:5-6

⁵ For the living know that they will die,
   but the dead know nothing;
they have no further reward,
   and even their name is forgotten.
⁶ Their love, their hate
   and their jealousy have long since vanished;
never again will they have a part
   in anything that happens under the sun.

In Time

Eyes will close
sickness will end
hearts will cease
fractures will mend

Love will calm
fears will subside
aches will vaporize
tears will dry

~ d², 06.26.21, 7:08 PM

The Space

Too crowded to
create
not by things,
but attachments

I need the
freedom
from responsibilities
deadlines
and
expectations

tunnel vision
lined with infinite boundaries

thoughts bouncing like
happy echoes
dissipating untouched

a bottomless pit of
possibilities
lit by my carefree
spark of inspiration
clinging to
boundless hope.

~ d², 06.26.21, 11:06 PM

Ecclesiastes 9:7-10

[7] Go, eat your food with gladness, and drink your wine with a joyful heart, for God has already approved what you do. [8] Always be clothed in white, and always anoint your head with oil. [9] Enjoy life with your wife, whom you love, all the days of this meaningless life that God has given you under the sun—all your meaningless days. For this is your lot in life and in your toilsome labor under the sun. [10] Whatever your hand finds to do, do it with all your might, for in the realm of the dead, where you are going, there is neither working nor planning nor knowledge nor wisdom.

Ecclesiastes 9:11-12

[11] I have seen something else under the sun:
The race is not to the swift
  or the battle to the strong,
nor does food come to the wise
  or wealth to the brilliant
  or favor to the learned;
but time and chance happen to them all.
[12] Moreover, no one knows when their hour will come:
As fish are caught in a cruel net,
  or birds are taken in a snare,
so people are trapped by evil times
  that fall unexpectedly upon them.

Scented Notes
Content Warning: Sexual Assault

Captured by memories locked and loaded,
scattered CliffNotes triggering volumes
abrupt recollections of memoirs
bringing the past to the very present, today

Like the ion-rich air after a brutal thunderstorm
attached to the sweet, dewy dampness of rain
pasted overalls clinging to a chilled body,
the joy of the moment scribbled on my brain

Like the scent of moist pennies,
gripped by sweaty fists jammed in tight pockets,
it is the leaking of an acrid wetness, framed
with traced evidence lingering on inspecting fingertips,
of when my menses unexpectedly came,
heavy with innocent shame

Like the day my mother vigorously cleaned
and ruined chitterlings for me,
there is not enough hot sauce, pepper sauce,
Tabasco, vinegar to coax me to eat,
Chile' I will never, never ever,
never, never ever crave that meat

Like the warmth of Kush oil
when inhaled, drunkenly comforts me
like palms cradling my velvety smooth
fresh moisturized face
fragrant molecules dabbed, sinking
embracing exposed and hidden pulse points
coaxing, rocking, swaying, soothing on beat

Ecclesiastes 9:11-12

a seductive melody of millennia-old memories
calling me, personally, perpetually, by my name

Like the smell etched into the walls
of peeling paint
hand-loomed woven threads
of a bed unmade,
soaked in custom-designed
light-blocking drapes,
deeply embedded in the keratin
in the shafts of loose braids

a thick smoke

exacerbating the wet welling
in a terrified gaze,
the haunting aroma of burnt cookies
still baking

while I was raped.

~ d^2, 09.29.22, 12:41 AM

Ecclesiastes 9:11-12

With Much Gusto

It's morning
time to wake up because it's

MORNING

what will I accomplish today
plans for a COOL project
coming my way
wait, what will I wear
love the clothes my closet bears
so many LOVELY colors
fresh water ready for me to hop
right in, my tub temperature is

GLORIOUS

my two-strand twist out is

FABULOUS

my platinum gray strands are simply

MARVELOUS

the aromatic scent of my oils
have me feeling powerful

SAUCY

and pure
check out my coordinating shoes
with the fresh peeking out
HOT red pedicure

excited about the two bottles of water grabbed,
walking out the door
I know that I will be parched NO MORE
WOW! The music as I hit the traffic is so smooth
this congestion allows a replay
of my jam, a time or two
I grab my tools and poised
to walk PROUDLY in the place
greeting my coworkers with a smiling face
sharing my joy in my imitable way

I SASHAY and parlay
my way to my cherished office space
bracing for the productivity
about to take place

LOVING my work is not wrong,
but it is time to play
will it be friends
or solitude to round out my day
both are equally rewarding
as the time floats away
then I longingly SWOON
looking googly-eyed
at my pillow
sinking in as my head
is perfectly cradles my head
luxuriating as I EASE
my eyes closed
until my alarm soars in a few hours and I once again
sing

MORNING!

~ d², 08.06.17, 12:41 AM

Ecclesiastes 9:11-12

Ecclesiastes 9:13-16

[13] I also saw under the sun this example of wisdom that greatly impressed me: [14] There was once a small city with only a few people in it. And a powerful king came against it, surrounded it and built huge siege works against it. [15] Now there lived in that city a man poor but wise, and he saved the city by his wisdom. But nobody remembered that poor man. [16] So I said,
"Wisdom is better than strength." But the poor man's wisdom is despised, and his words are no longer heeded.

Flossing

Some folks will
chew you up
extract all
the vital juices
spit you out

then

get mad at you for the
lingering flesh
stuck between
their teeth

~ d^2, 06.22.19, 5:10 PM

Sight Beyond Sight

Ecclesiastes 9:13-16

Focus undone
to protect the story

Weary but
unbranded glory

Undreamable scenarios
viewed
without knowing

Ties to heart strings
with unraveled
apprehension showing

Soft shelter
grinded harsh

Notes from a
saxophone
crooning a
farce

Illegally longing
for
a righteous intent

Feeding a thirst
for energy
spent

Oh
the yearning

Ecclesiastes 9:13-16

for vision
stable

Met instead with
passion
sacrificed on the
table

Unobscured by
cataracted
promises
lost and found

Like a heartbeat
missing
in the ultrasound

Stigmatized by
careless decisions

Dismayed by the
editor's revisions

Blindfolded
by the cheese
in the traps

Beads of
chained jewelry
snapped

Bouncing rhythmically in deep unsearchable cracks—

Bouncing...
Rhythmically...
In...
Deep...
Unsearchable...
Cracks...

Mazes too intricate
to navigate
alone

A hearth too
narrow
for the plaque
"Home Sweet Home"

Pulsating warmth
compressed damp
with support

Facing a
biased judge
in court

Easing emotional migraines
piercing the picture

A garish
hot yellow
naive
future

Ecclesiastes 9:13-16

Ecclesiastes 9:13-16

Mouths spewing
obscenities
immune to the
threat of soap

Heralding a past
flourishing with
redemptive hope

Shackled
to the present
the exhaustive joy

Self-indulgent
leisure
a collector's
priceless toy

And a future
inches
away,
locked with
a misplaced key

The siren song
skims the lazy
ripples of the sea

Seeking refuge in the
folds
of your ear

Novels of expectations
wasted in unshed tears

Coaxing peace and a
pregnant
connection

Hedging all bets
to be the
exception

Begging
oh so
silently

Just
to be
clearly
seen

~ d², 07.22.14, 11:57 PM

Ecclesiastes 9:13-16

Ecclesiastes 9:17-18

¹⁷ The quiet words of the wise are more to be heeded
 than the shouts of a ruler of fools.
¹⁸ Wisdom is better than weapons of war,
 but one sinner destroys much good.

Fly Strip

Wisdom is the
equivalent of freshly spun honey

can accomplish more
than might or money

~ d^2, 08.06.17, 1:16 PM

The Book of Ecclesiastes, Chapter 10

Living the struggle is only glamorous in retrospect.

9.24.22, "The Return"

Imprisoned Minds

Bodies shift, and twist
through tunnels
of time, breaking through
cocoons, to incrementally
build strength, muscles wrapped around
bones, stretching to reach
levels, achievements and then breaking
down, retracting to wither and
shrink, boring through
minerals, leaving holes to
weaken, caging a resolute and ever
sharp mind, reverberating a voice
that is mine, spewing out commands
registering, responses with varying
stunted readiness

~ d^2, 11.29.22, 10:34 PM

Ecclesiastes 10:1

[1]As dead flies give perfume a bad smell, so a little folly outweighs wisdom and honor.

Ecclesiastes 10:2

[2] *The heart of the wise inclines to the right, but the heart of the fool to the left.*

To Engineer

is knowing
that there is
not one way
but that you need
to evaluate
multiple ways
to determine
the best way
then commit
to developing
the way
to materialize
that way
while being open
to one day
having to upgrade
to a better way
or throw it all away
to devise a new way

~ d², 08.29.22, 2:58 PM

Feeding

I scroll down
my screen

and read
thoughts and ideas

a vast variety

revealing over time
consistent themes

and the prominent
is the oblivious jackal
attached to their reactionary fools

those who clamor to
become "pick me" support

or

those who
chose to be contrary
     they like to fight

Don't taste and see...
spit out in disgust

allow them room to
showcase their
colorful plumes
without falling through their
contagious vortex

Ecclesiastes 10:3

³ *Even as fools walk along the road,*
  they lack sense
    and show everyone how stupid they are.

Ecclesiastes 10:3

scroll, swipe, wipe, and wave

past the clown parade

jesters on display

and smile at their
dark comedic
brand of
enjoyment

~ d², 10.26.23, 11:46 PM

It's Not Personal, It's Business

We assume roles
attached to goals
once obtained
    are converted to
        tender
products of exchange
for profit
organized to meet
a desired
bottom line

each level answers
to a whip-cracked
and an expectation
that must be met
the weight of it can often
press emotions
and those lacking
can lash out
to those beneath

but it is about the goal
not personalities
even when colored approaches
guide

focus on the goal
not the attitude

protect your space with
healthy boundaries
in place

Ecclesiastes 10:4

*4 If a ruler's anger rises against you,
do not leave your post;
calmness can lay great offenses to rest.*

Ecclesiastes 10:4

allow them to
take a beat

room to vent
once

and
sometimes repeat

empathize realities
of concurrently served masters
and adjust

pull in what is sincere
keep your overall purpose clear

and it will become
a safe, secure, and trusted
occupational rest

~ d², 10.27.23, 8:36 PM

The Negro

I was born Negro,
    in an era where it was celebrated not to be
    considered colored

I was born Negro,
    in a time when the strides of the 60s were the
    new world order

I was born Negro,
    while movie houses still had sections to keep
    social order

I was born Negro,
    when it was still a fatal risk to talk to the other

I was born Negro,
    just five years after my parents were arrested at
    a counter

I was born Negro,
    when an Afro pick and blue hair grease were
    sold for a buck and a quarter

I was born Negro,
    when the stench of burnt bodies hung on
    twisted twine was still a looming horror

~ d², 09.20.22, 10:34 PM

Ecclesiastes 10:5-7

[5] There is an evil I have seen under the sun,
    the sort of error that arises from a ruler:

[6] Fools are put in many high positions,
    while the rich occupy the low ones.
[7] I have seen slaves on horseback,
    while princes go on foot like slaves.

Ecclesiastes 10:8-9

*8 Whoever digs a pit may fall into it;
  whoever breaks through a wall may be bitten by a snake.*

*9 Whoever quarries stones may be injured by them;
  whoever splits logs may be endangered by them.*

I Woke Up

From unconscious
to conscious breathing
I woke up
this morning
dressed,
    hoped
        for a new day

But,
wore an illicit outfit
too much skin
too alluring
end result,
brutal rape

Woke up
this morning
transformed wardrobe,
    hoped
        for a new day

But,
allowed
no's to be ignored
by an insistent
entitled date

Woke up
this morning
changed
my voice,
    hoped
        for a new day

Ecclesiastes 10:8-9

But,
chattered
too much sass
he had to put
me back
into my place

Woke up
this morning
silenced my voice,
>   hoped
>   for a new day

But,
stood in the
wrong place
as his fist
crashed into face

Woke up this morning
ran,
>   hoped
>   for a new day

But,
the violation of
leaving the scene
is contained
within an
unmarked grave

Ecclesiastes 10:8-9

Woke up
this morning
searched closet,
    braced
        for a new day

But,
layered in
corrupt colors
vulnerable to bullets
draped
multihued in blood red

Woke up
this morning
updated outfit,
    braced
        for a new day

But,
by donning an
incorrect size
ill-fitted for
decent society
there is
decaying flesh
wantonly discarded

Woke up
this morning
harmonized legitimate garments,
    braced
        for a new day

But,
spoke
without humility
uppity voice is now
regretfully
dead

Woke up
this morning
upgraded language,
    braced
        for a new day

But,
conversed too proper
while my back
wears a "X" as a
friendly fire
target

Woke up
this morning
switched zip codes,
    braced
        for a new day

Ecclesiastes 10:8-9

Ecclesiastes 10:8-9

But,
the unwanted
presence,
gift-wrapped
boxed chattel,
threatens and
spooks
neighbors
locked and
loaded

Woke up
this morning
crawling,
    cried
        in a new day

But,
screaming was so loud
mommy quiets
with multiple shakes so violent

Woke up
this morning
cooed,
    cried
        in a new day

But,
volume and tone
annoyed daddy
he used my arm as an ashtray

Woke up
this morning
rolled over,
    cried
        in a new day

But,
a soiled diaper
neglectfully untouched
until bedsores
ate at strength

Woke up
this morning
sat up,
    cried
        in a new day

But,
was unable to hold breath
long enough
my little body is immersed in water
still laid

Woke up
this morning
dreamed I was
not guilty of my death

Ecclesiastes 10:8-9

Ecclesiastes 10:8-9

But,
power and privilege
made a compelling case
against innocence
shame married to
responsibility lingers in
the last sour breath

cause...

I woke up

~ d², 11.12.14, 4:44 PM

To-Do

I have a list
of un-delegatable tasks
that is if I just
canceled out rest,
    grind it
      non-stop

I would mark them
done

In theory, I am just that good
In reality, after 24 hours production degrades
the capacity of my brain
to function

my vast skills start to dwindle
the spark of my brilliance
refuses to kindle

until my efforts
are a waste
so I grudgingly collapse
and rest
with utter exhaustion, lest
I continue with a pace
with one-half faulty measure

    (If only I would add consistent restorative rest so
    I would always perform with excellence)

    ~ d², 10.27.23, 9:45 PM

Ecclesiastes 10:10

¹⁰ If the ax is dull
    and its edge unsharpened,
more strength is needed,
    but skill will bring success.

Ecclesiastes 10:11

[11] *If a snake bites before it is charmed, the charmer receives no fee.*

To-Do, to Be Continued

I am no good
if I do not
rest

I am skilled but
my excellence
is rarely met without
first being at my
best

I disappoint more
than I want to
confess

when I leave my basic needs unmet

I lose out on more than my
parasitic efforts
can get

refunds
must be sent

my good reputation
spent

I am always needing to
repent

folks never know
what to expect

my deadlines
always slip

So, I need to underpromise
overdeliver
after I
undercommit
and overrest

I need to deliver for myself
before
I can deliver to others, what is left.

~ d². 10.27.23, 9:45 PM

Ecclesiastes 10:11

Ecclesiastes 10:12-15

[12] Words from the mouth of the wise are gracious,
    but fools are consumed by their own lips.
[13] At the beginning their words are folly;
    at the end they are wicked madness—

[14]   and fools multiply words.
No one knows what is coming—
    who can tell someone else what will happen after them?

[15] The toil of fools wearies them;
    they do not know the way to town.

The Waves

Riding on the waves
of this moment
focus established epicenter of
    concentric circles
that flow in and out of that axis
the central moment
first drawing in tightly
your emotions
then expanding out, like invasive tentacles
    to those who share
the same focus
occasionally sparking contact beyond the
    walls of your familiar cocoon
    to take notice
of those outside and
make mention
postings
then drawing again, back in
and out to comfortable others
in and out
with turbulences ebbing and
    flowing based on
the recollection of weighted memories
and that staggering empty notice
unpredictable, but noticed

~ d^2, 09.20.22, 10:34 PM

Shall I Compare Thee...
A nod to Sonnet 18 by William Shakespeare

    Shall I compare thee to a lonely child

    You are a separate being from
        the whole world

    Sought things do not gather you to a
        belonging place

    Nor empty praise providing a pat
        on the head

    Your quest is wrought with missed cues
        and turns

    Liars and cheats beguile you with their words

    I shake with dread for the trauma deep
        within your folds

~ d², 01.09.23

Ecclesiastes 10:16-17

[16] Woe to the land whose king was a servant
   and whose princes feast in the morning.
[17] Blessed is the land whose king is of noble birth
   and whose princes eat at a proper time—
   for strength and not for drunkenness.

Ecclesiastes 10:18

18 Through laziness, the rafters sag; because of idle hands, the house leaks.

Some Folks

Sometimes,
folks who say they are waiting
are avoiding

Sometimes,
folks who say they need rest
are engaging in neglect

Sometimes,
folks who say they are contemplating
are frozen and confused

Sometimes,
folks who say they are giving deference
are cowards

Sometimes,
folks who say they are making room
are abdicating responsibility

Sometimes,
folks who say they steadfast
are really stuck

Sometimes,
folks who say they are reserved
are insecure

Sometimes,
folks who say they are fasting
are really broke

Sometimes,
folks who say they are giving
are often used

Sometimes,
folks who say they are at fault
are really victims of abuse

Sometimes,
the folks who say these things
are me

~ d², 10.27.23, 10:53 PM

Ecclesiastes 10:18

Ecclesiastes 10:19

99 A feast is made for laughter, wine makes life merry, and money is the answer for everything.

With or Without Means

These three things
    Your Community
    Your Joy
    And Your Means

How they are combined shows our ability to obtain internal peace

No community, no joy, with no means:
can lead to depression and death

No community, no joy, with means:
renders its owner empty success

No community, with joy, and no means:
can cause hope to leave

No community, with joy, and means:
can lead to an insatiable greed

Community, with no joy, and no means:
feeling alone in the crowd

Community, with no joy, and means:
people pleasing can abound

Community, with joy, and no means:
the objects of a charity to feed

Community, with joy, and means:
all shall have what they need

~ d² 10.31.23, 2:09 PM

Gradients

Humanity is
wrapped in
countless spectrums
percentage points
from
divine perfection
toward
the closer perfect fool
for that which is not
in complete collusion
offers up play for consideration
wisdom proceeds down
each graph
while opposing apathy
tempers tongues
weakening entitlements

~ d², 08.06.17, 2:28 AM

Ecclesiastes 10:20

[20] *Do not revile the king even in your thoughts,
    or curse the rich in your bedroom,
because a bird in the sky may carry your words,
    and a bird on the wing may report what you say.*

The Book of Ecclesiastes, Chapter 11

Called for This

Laser pointed firmly on my

target

a goal with solid steps

measured

moments prudently organized and

planned

to move as required to get the job

done

are the days of aimless

activity

has a solid purpose, a life beckoning others to

eternity

is our reward for a belief in God who knows

everything

happens solely in Jehovah's time and

reasoning

Ashé and Amen.

~ d², 08.06.17, 3:16 AM

Ecclesiastes 11:1-6

[1] Ship your grain across the sea;
    after many days you may receive a return.
[2] Invest in seven ventures, yes, in eight;
    you do not know what disaster may come upon the land.
[3] If clouds are full of water,
    they pour rain on the earth.
Whether a tree falls to the south or to the north,
    in the place where it falls, there it will lie.
[4] Whoever watches the wind will not plant;
    whoever looks at the clouds will not reap.
[5] As you do not know the path of the wind,
    or how the body is formed[a] in a mother's womb,
so you cannot understand the work of God,
    the Maker of all things.
[6] Sow your seed in the morning,
    and at evening let your hands not be idle,
for you do not know which will succeed,
    whether this or that,
    or whether both will do equally well.

Ecclesiastes 11:7-10

⁷ Light is sweet,
   and it pleases the eyes to see the sun.
⁸ However many years anyone may live,
   let them enjoy them all.
But let them remember the days of darkness,
   for there will be many.
   Everything to come is meaningless.
⁹ You who are young, be happy while you are young,
   and let your heart give you joy in the days of your youth.
Follow the ways of your heart
   and whatever your eyes see,
but know that for all these things
   God will bring you into judgment.
¹⁰ So then, banish anxiety from your heart
   and cast off the troubles of your body,
   for youth and vigor are meaningless.

Betrothed

Treasuring
each second

Mounting
in minutes

Forging
into hours

Wearing
daily commitment

Coupling
in activities of your youth

Binding
the pledge of old age

Unifying
a dwindling calendar

Fearing
no one
but God

while engaged

~ d², 08.06.17, 4:50 AM

The Book of Ecclesiastes, Chapter 12

You always have a choice in the matter. You do not have the right to dictate the consequences.

9.24.22, "The End Result"

At All Times

Be vigilant in your
pleasure
be mindful of the
source
be aware
that all you do
will be judged
encouraging seedlings to grow
for new buds
need fresh water

~ d², 08.06.17, 5:49 AM

Ecclesiastes 12:1-8

*¹ Remember your Creator
   in the days of your youth,
before the days of trouble come
   and the years approach when you will say,
   "I find no pleasure in them"—
² before the sun and the light
   and the moon and the stars grow dark,
   and the clouds return after the rain;
³ when the keepers of the house tremble,
   and the strong men stoop,
when the grinders cease because they are few,
   and those looking through the windows grow dim;
⁴ when the doors to the street are closed
   and the sound of grinding fades;
when people rise up at the sound of birds,
   but all their songs grow faint;
⁵ when people are afraid of heights
   and of dangers in the streets;
when the almond tree blossoms
   and the grasshopper drags itself along
   and desire no longer is stirred.
Then people go to their eternal home
   and mourners go about the streets.
⁶ Remember him—before the silver cord is severed,
   and the golden bowl is broken;
before the pitcher is shattered at the spring,
   and the wheel broken at the well,
⁷ and the dust returns to the ground it came from,
   and the spirit returns to God who gave it.
⁸ "Meaningless! Meaningless!" says the Teacher.
   "Everything is meaningless!"*

Ecclesiastes 12:1-8

The Irreducible

Can I... this moment...
just choose
to be

positioned supine while
coasting between the
layers of an inconspicuously
silent ringing
nothingness

languishing within empty
complete thoughts
heaped together piles of
overflowing baskets of
unsorted garments
spilling to the floor
setting traps to
trip up my steps out the door
seeking to condemn me to
infinite degrees of trifling
that I resoundingly reject

joyfully

treasured neglect is my beloved pet
curled up
warming my lap
snoring a tune
beguiling invisible expectations
mindlessly savoring the prize of existence
swiftly dismissing
the definition of
an "is"

Ecclesiastes 12:1-8

inhaling transparently
obscure indulgences
exhaling discarded
unaddressed concerns
into piles of careless dishes
shamelessly unrinsed
or guiltlessly unsorted

They will be okay until... naw
They will be okay

I just want to spend this moment
marveling in the wonder of
a chest rising and falling
indiscriminately

soaking in the base
rich blessing

that foundational
Holy and sacred element

Oh, the divine glory for
I am alive

For that alone
I humbly give
my greatest of thanks

~ d², 01.10.23, 5:22 PM

Ecclesiastes 12:9-10

[9] Not only was the Teacher wise, but he also imparted knowledge to the people. He pondered and searched out and set in order many proverbs. [10] The Teacher searched to find just the right words, and what he wrote was upright and true.

How and Why I Poet

In the beginning
there is a seed
planted by a vapor
elegantly wisping through cracks
in my busyness
and packed calendar

forcing me to pause breathing
stale uninspired air
switching to don my mask
to inhale
life

discovered through words

traveling from seductive thoughts
and then through to fingers
scribbles typed or written
themes captured in their succinct
totality

jumbles of notions that
arrest the ability to expand my lungs
rise my chest
open my throat
and speak
a silence, unintelligible
but brilliant

grasping incomplete concepts
structured holding patterns
circling low to the ground

waiting to land
until
the clock resumes
and the moment before
the tick of the movement of
the second hand

I ready my breath
to exhale
something divinely fresh
and new.

~ d², 09.06.22, 11:54 PM

Ecclesiastes 12:9-10

Ecclesiastes 12:11-12a

[11] *The words of the wise are like goads, their collected sayings like firmly embedded nails—given by one shepherd.[b] 12 Be warned, my son, of anything in addition to them. Of making many books there is no end, and much study wearies the body.*

A Case for a Goodnight

Today, I woke up late
decided to protect my peace
at all costs

I sat in the bed longer
than I intended
and had zero remorse

I scrolled on my phone
avoiding my inbox for hours

I kept my phone on silent
pressed snooze more than once

I inhaled my autonomy and exhaled,
sharply, out all expectations

not today

Today, I wanted to simmer
and marinate on decisions encased in
hidden entries on my calendar
longer than recommended

I wanted all of that time to focus
on breathing without purpose
it is what it is,
absent the scientific explanations

It is just a thing
that takes place
over and over
usually ignored, but

Today, I took notice
and instead of weaving projects
of significance between the marks I
sat and took notice
the sound orchestrated
in that momentary pause

My mind bounced casually
on the riding of stilted time
swaying to a rhythm
uniquely mine
entertaining irritations
of allowed interruptions
regretting them
almost immediately

I decoded my capitulation as weakness
and I sighed,
daring to next time
strengthen my resolve
for my whirlwind of exceptions
has accelerated its
wind

The frenzy is now so high,
three hours after midnight
it is way past time
I just took my dose of melatonin
I need to call it a night

~ d², 09.13.22, 3:43 AM

Ecclesiastes 12:11-12a

Ecclesiastes 12:13-14

[13] Now all has been heard;
   here is the conclusion of the matter:
Fear God and keep his commandments,
   for this is the duty of all mankind.
[14] For God will bring every deed into judgment,
   including every hidden thing,
   whether it is good or evil.

As Qoheleth Admires The Truth

Captured in the
commandments
bathed in righteousness

God is Righteousness

human reach
captures a mere
portion of love

God is Love

expanding to touch us all

God is Counselor

God is Comforter

leaving etchings in our hearts
as pure foundation

God is Source

while shifting nonsense
makes room for knowledge

God is Truth

the awe of the beauty
of a God we cannot see

God is Omnipresent

complex layers
never fully reveal

God is Omniscient

how amazing is The Divine

God is Omnipotent

birthed from no one
yet
eternally
still

God Is

~ d², 08.06.17, 6:20 AM

Ecclesiastes 12:13-14

Ecclesiastes

What if she knew that her heart was the source of her magic? Spinning spells of intricate alchemy inducing forever trances, revealing with its true beauty defined by the intoxicating wine of time independent of fraudulent adornments. What if she knew?

Click My Heels

Call me
old fashioned,
but
I like to send out
thank you notes

A polite and proper
gesture
that communicates
how one appreciates
that gift to me from you

The note should
acknowledge the
full
specifics of that
which was given
and describe the
full
value of that
which was received

An affirming declaration of
how You blessed me

Thank You...

For that
metaphysical
invisible string
between
two cans empty
reach

Ecclesiastes

Ecclesiastes

that took years
to weave and construct
so to complete
the connection

For
igniting weathered kindling
doused
with salt-watered,
translucent
ramblings, and
long-lost,
hopeless
dissertations

For
guiding toward
The Light
through a darkness
so heavy
I was left lingering
in a deafening
visual uncertainty
of lids being
open or closed

For
revealing
the combination
for me to calm
my own storm

For
viewing
the candid
exhibition
of my abstract
interpretation
of raw
feminine
expression
and seeing it
as art

For
being the welcoming
Deep Valley
warmly embracing
the reverberating echoes of my
cries, moans, and screams
then
sending them back
musically
tenderly

For
fostering my
orphaned spirit
until it was secured and
deemed fit to
move back and
enmesh with my soul

Ecclesiastes

Ecclesiastes

For
the space to connect
with abandoned and
discarded memories
and the freedom to
caress
my intellect
with the
extracted remnants
of goodness
and with mercy

For
the ability to
mature
my emotions
from the
necessary lessons
contained within the
lingering dross[1]

For
breathing
the hope of
a potential
beat of life
into my heart

---

[1] Dross: 1: metallurgy : the scum or unwanted material that forms on the surface of molten metal. 2: waste or foreign matter : IMPURITY. 3: something that is base, trivial, or inferior

Ecclesiastes

For
the necessary silence
to hear my own voice

For
balancing out
an unbalanced admiration

For
handing me a shovel
as I excavated through
trauma-enriched soil
that nurtured my
comfortable state
of mediocrity

For
being my Ride and Die
and Rise
as I cleared out the
chaotic debris
of
once valuable
trinkets
now crushed and
reduced to
a mound of
totally
insignificant
rubble

Ecclesiastes

For
inspecting the uniquely
placed forms
tailor-made for
my personality
and temperament
before
Your Divine foundation
was poured

For
being the scaffolding
as the skeleton structure
was erected
then
gracefully
removing it
so I could
skillfully tend
to the
aesthetic placement
of the brick & mortar
of my new existence

For
providing
validating and
entertaining
channels of focus
until it was time to
remotely
power them down

and allow the heat to
casually dissipate
until the surface,
to the touch,
was cold

For
helping me
redefine what it means
to be at home

There is no place like it...

Home

> "Perhaps home is not a place but simply an irrevocable condition."
> —James Baldwin, *Giovanni's Room*
>
> ~ d², 08.04.13

Ecclesiastes

Ecclesiastes 12:9-14

⁹ Not only was the Teacher wise, but he also imparted knowledge to the people. He pondered and searched out and set in order many proverbs. ¹⁰ The Teacher searched to find just the right words, and what he wrote was upright and true.

¹¹ The words of the wise are like goads, their collected sayings like firmly embedded nails—given by one shepherd. ¹² Be warned, my son, of anything in addition to them. Of making many books there is no end, and much study wearies the body.

¹³ Now all has been heard;
  here is the conclusion of the matter:
Fear God and keep his commandments,
  for this is the duty of all mankind.
¹⁴ For God will bring every deed into judgment,
  including every hidden thing,
  whether it is good or evil.

Epilogue: A Second Look

Exposure
creating space
to touch truth
faith
holding space
to mature
knowing
clears up space
opening up measures of time
study
with purpose divine
not
the ego of mind
in all things
still
hold up God
in reverential fear
for no action
through
word
emotion
motivation
inclination
inspiration
anticipation
or recreation
is secret
to God all
will be revealed

~ d², 08.06.17, 8:56 AM

Qoheleth, THE TEACHER
Qoheleth, MY MUSE

My Father's Reprise

Daddy's Home

I was spoiled rotten as a child.

Not with things, per se, but with love.

I never doubted that my parents, Frances Jeanette Barcroft Dalton and Robert Bernard Dalton, loved and adored one extremely precious and adorable Deborah Lynn Dalton.

I also grew up with an unshakable reality that Daddy was always coming home.

My father was in the military. Retired after 26 years of service as a Lieutenant Colonel in the US Army. As a combat rescue helicopter pilot in the early Vietnam years, he served in some very risky tours/missions. It was not until I was an adult, when he finally shared his stories, that I fully understood how blessed I was to have that unwavering assurance.

It did not matter if the time was just the average workday hours, days away on a weekend drill, weeks on assignments, or months hidden away on foreign soil...

Daddy was always coming home.

When his keys jingled at the door, and his strong footsteps came across the threshold, the joy and excitement expressed in our household was akin to winning a multi-state, multimillion-dollar lottery.

Daddy was now home, and all was right in our world.

My Father's Reprise

My Father's Reprise

I remember vividly the last time I was privileged to look into his eyes, sit on his lap, hug him with all of my might, and nuzzle my head on his shoulders (as any good Daddy's Little Girl would do) knowing this was the last time I would be able to enjoy that type of intimate father-daughter tenderness.

Although my father's once muscular and large frame was now small, fragile, and frail due to the two competing cancers raging violently through his body, the strength of his love for me oozed through his arms, words, and heart as he held his Little Pumpkin one last time.

Daddy was no longer going to be coming home.

I was conflicted with a profound sadness and the joy of knowing I was able to bask, for the last time, in my daddy's presence.

At his wake, I defiantly protested viewing his body, as he had specifically directed.

He wanted to be quickly cremated after his death, with his ashes thrown somewhere. He said this planet is to be used by the living. No need to waste valuable space for the dead.

He taught me that the flesh and bone shell dressed up in his full military regalia was no longer where he, the true essence of him, lived.

And he was right.

My Father's Reprise

My daughters wanted one last view, so, to support them, I went, and my brief glimpse confirmed what he pointedly taught.

That was his body, but Daddy was not there. Daddy was not home. He was never coming back home, not there.

All I sensed was a heavy, dark emptiness that left me cold and woefully uncomforted.

When I walked them outside of the building to play with their newly introduced cousins, I looked out at the sky, breathed in the night air, and was shaken by the intimate connection I felt, but I could not properly describe The What that I was connected to.

I just knew that, with each breath, I felt more at peace. With each sigh, I felt more at home. It was not a strange sensation—I had felt that way before.

It was the same comfort, love, and peace that I felt when I was nestled in my father's arms.

It was years later, in a Bible study inspired by the novel *The Shack*—when the specific session focused on the present day spiritual encounters of the living with deceased loved ones, I fully understood what took place.

The evening after his wake, at my Daddy's funeral in my public remarks while his urn sat prominently in the center of the sanctuary, I labeled the sensations felt as his spirit comforting me. Just like a good daddy should. But during this lesson, God revealed to me that it was much bigger than just an

My Father's Reprise

acknowledgment of the greatness of Robert Bernard Dalton. During the study focus of the day, our pastor (The Reverend Dr. Robert C. Scott, Senior Pastor at St. Paul Baptist Church, Charlotte, NC) shared two Bible verses that grabbed my heart with such strength that the sacred words forcefully coaxed out an undeniable proper context.

Although I had a rational love of God, I still held on to some lingering bitterness toward God that made it a challenge to properly process the sadness felt years after my father's death.

Romans 8:28 NKJV
"And we know that all things work together for good to those who love God, to those who are the called according to His purpose."

When I heard him read this in relation to the death of my father, I was pissed.

How in the world could my father's dying be something good?

Yeah, yeah, I remembered the rote rhetoric I quoted from the pulpit at his funeral about appreciating the gift of time we had after almost losing him 11 years earlier through illness.

I appreciated the blessing of 11 years more. But, dammit, I still wanted his physical body here, now.

I was recovering from my third miscarriage, tired of death and loss. I wanted my Daddy. I wanted the comfort found in his arms.

My Father's Reprise

How could any of this be good? Seriously, God, how?

Then, Pastor directed us to The Message Version, expanding it out to the two verses before:

Romans 8:26-28 NKJV
> *"Meanwhile, the moment we get tired in the waiting, God's Spirit is right alongside helping us along. If we don't know how or what to pray, it doesn't matter. He does our praying in and for us, making prayer out of our wordless sighs, our aching groans. He knows us far better than we know ourselves, knows our pregnant condition, and keeps us present before God. That's why we can be so sure that every detail in our lives of love for God is worked into something good."*

Then, Pastor took us to **James 1:16-18 The Message Version:**
> *"So, my very dear friends, don't get thrown off course. Every desirable and beneficial gift comes out of heaven. The gifts are rivers of light cascading down from the Father of Light. There is nothing deceitful in God, nothing two-faced, nothing fickle. He brought us to life using the true Word, showing us off as the crown of all his creatures."*

I was equally stunned, humbled, and exhilarated!

It wasn't that the spirit of my father was present and loving me after his death—rather it was God present and loving me through my father while he, Daddy, was alive.

My Father's Reprise

All of the goodness that I was longing for from my daddy, was really the goodness that came from God. It was only through the death of my daddy, that I was broken enough to now know that I was ready to receive it directly from the original source.

I am grateful to God for gifting me with a loving, caring, supportive, sarcastic, humorous, and compassionate father.

It was through the joy of seeing him come home as a child that I was able to fully appreciate the God who has always been here.

Qoheleth, THE TEACHER
Qoheleth, MY MUSE

Afterword

Carl W. Kenney II

> *"Poetry is when an emotion has found its thought and the thought has found words,"* said Robert Frost (1874 – 1963), an American poet known for exploring questions of existence and themes of loneliness in an uncaring world.

Frost's definition of poetry illustrates the deep grappling of *Qoheleth, the Teacher/ Qoheleth, My Muse*, Deborah Dalton's reflections on the words of the son of David, king of Jerusalem.

"Vanity of vanities! All is futile!" is the existential question Qoheleth ponders. Life is not enough. It vanishes too quickly. It is like a vapor, ending in death for both the wise and foolish.

Dalton confronts the meaning of life transcendent of the burden of living and the assumptions of good living. Beyond convictions involving judgment, reward, and God's will—what does it all mean?

Like a scribe of the ancient Jewish tradition, Dalton studies and interprets the Book of Ecclesiastes with a will to uncover the mystery of the text. She applies both exegesis, the tools of critical interpretation, and eisegesis, the review of the text guided by her own experiences. Exegesis considers Qoheleth's context and understanding of meaning. Eisegesis relates how the text influences Dalton's own understanding of meaning.

Dalton effectively weaves her calling as a poet with her theological training to blend scholarship, Bible Study, and meditation. Dalton rouses the memory of Teresa of Avilla (1515-1582). Avila's Interior Castle imagined the soul's traveling through a castle with seven chambers. Dalton offers a mysticism with Ecclesiastes as a tool shifting the soul from the agonizing wrestling with earthly meaning toward answers in poems inspired by Qoheleth's assessment of life.

Dalton provides a version of modern-day mysticism within a tradition seeking union with God through deep contemplation and surrender. She uses poetry, study, and spiritual discernment to create words and thoughts to express emotions.

"I wish that I could expertly paint a picture that evoked an emotion so guttural that when those who gaze upon its visage, a reluctant tear of bittersweet melancholy would carelessly fail," Dalton evokes in "The Pointless Promise", in response to Ecclesiastes 2:1-3.

"But that would be meaningless."

"Whether or not I lose these 50 pounds
It is all meaningless

Whether or not I buy myself the perfectly appointed new house
It is meaningless" Dalton continues in a series of assertions prodding the complex nature of living.

But there's more.

"I sigh
I am alive
And I have the world available to me as a beautiful promise.
But, it is all meaningless," Dalton concludes.

Each poem is a plea to consider meaning beyond the simplistic remedies expounded in many contemporary pulpits. The quest for meaning often hinders the soul's movement toward liberation from a life of futility.

Dalton engages readers to ponder a more enlightened way. What is the meaning of life beyond death? Where is the overcoming for women frustrated by the unfulfilled expectations rooted in a theology of a woman's submission?

"What do workers gain from their toil?" Qoheleth asks in Ecclesiastes 3:9-14.

Dalton offers meditation moving readers beyond the dismay of living.

"ordained paths
parting through a sea of naysayers
leaving room to
humbly march onward
leaving only

> *personal mountains*
> *of embedded treachery*
> *to comb through*
> *begging to release*
> *nits grabbing hold of roots,"* Dalton offers in a section of "What is for You, Is for You."

Each poems responds to the angst and joy of Qoheleth's wisdom literature. Dalton challenges readers to enjoy the simple pleasures of life—to enjoy all of God's gifts. The gift of Dalton's work is in placing the wisdom of this ageless book within today's context. She brings life into words often overlooked by altering experiences. Dalton brings her personal encounter with the text to renew the wisdom of the original contribution.

This is a message for today embedded in the perpetual search for meaning in a life with ambiguous purpose. Dalton wrestles with a word acclaimed for being relevant yesterday, today, and forevermore.

This is the word of God within the word of God. This is fresh breath arousing hope while challenged by questions involving faith. These are poems for people perplexed by anxiety and dread. This is the witness for people seeking answers after the questions beyond the questions no longer feed the soul.

Anselm of Canterbury (1033-1109) says theology is "faith seeking understanding." Dalton's poems are theology supreme. This is her dialogue with the truths in the text while seeking understanding when faith dwindles due to the burden of living.

Dalton engages in a conversation with a wisdom poet involving theodicy—the answer to why a good God permits evil.

What is the meaning of life?
Where is God when I need more than this?

> *"I am ignorant to the*
> *wisdom*
> *It must possess,"* Dalton states in "The Unheard Melody"

There are numerous questions to explore. There is wisdom beyond the God of our understanding. What happens when knowing God is challenged by unexplained human experiences?

Dalton offers a unique conversation with the grappling of a wisdom poet. She brings both her mind and her heart. The spirit touches her imagination. Words explode on pages to reveal her faith seeking greater understanding.

These are poems.

This is a theological treatise.

This is mysticism.

This is a collection of meditations.

More than that, this is the word of God, for the people of God.

Thanks be to God.

Carl W. Kenney II
Hussman School of Journalism & Media, Assistant Professor

Durham Voice, Editor-in-Chief

Black Thought Media LLC
Publisher & Editor-in-Chief at Durham Rev-elution

Black Pearl Media Works, Co-Producer
God of the Oppressed,
an independent documentary film on
Black Liberation and Womanist theologies

Liberation Station
A Black Faith Think Tank
Convener of the Rev-elution
May 2023

BIBLIOGRAPHY

Baldwin, James, Vintage Book, a Divison of Random House, LLC, a Penguin Random House Company, New York, 1956, 1984, 2013.

Brown, William P., Interpretations, a Bible Commentary for teaching and preaching, Eccelesiasstes, Westminster John Knox Press, Louisville, KY, 2011.

Gottwald, Norman K., The Hebrew Bible: A Socio-Literary Introduction, Fortress Press, Philadelphia, PA, 1985

Hondru, Joyce, E(EEK)CCLESIASTES: Finding Meaning in a Meaningless Life, HarperCollins Christian Publishing, Nashville, TN, 2018.

Leong, T. F., Our Reason for Being: An Exposition of Ecclesiastes on the Meaning of Life, Wipf and Stock Publishers, Eugene, OR, 2022.

Longman, Tremper III, The New International Commentary on the Old Testament: The Book of Ecclesiastes, Wm. B. Eerdmans Publishing Co., Grand Rapids, MI, 1998.

Meek, Russell L., Ecclesiastes and the Search for Meaning in an Upside-Down World, Hendrickson Publishers, Peabody, MA, 2022.

Wiersbe, Warren W., Be Satisfied (Ecclesiastes) Looing for the Answer to the Meaning of Life, David C. Cook Publishing, Colorado Springs, CO, 2010, Second Edition.

Wolfe, Lisa M., Qoheleth (Ecclesisates), A Micheal Glazier Book by Liturgical Press, Collegeville, MN, Brenner-Idan (volume editor), Athalya, Reid Barbara E. (general editor), 2020.

ACKNOWLEDGMENTS

I could not have completed this book alone. I have been overwhelmingly blessed by so many while bringing this project to a close.

I received my first motivation to start while participating in my first 24 Hour Poetry Marathon in 2017. Many, many thanks to the founders of this engaging platform that has been inspiring poets to push themselves for over 8 years.

I want to thank my Community Literature Initiative family. Our weekly meetings since September 2022 were more than just a class session, they were the building of a family that I will hold dear to my heart for many years to come.

So many thanks to my loving community that extends to encompass all that I came across while attending The University of Arkansas at Pine Bluff, Lawrence Institute of Technology (Southfield, MI), Prairie View A&M University (Prairie View, TX), Eden Theological Seminary (Webster, MO), Trinity Episcopal Church (Pine Bluff, AR), The Church Without Walls (Houston, TX), Central Baptist Church (St. Louis, MO), St. Paul Baptist Church (Charlotte, NC), and my private social media groups (US Family, Lighthouse Family, and the Poetry Marathon Family). And finally, my Delta Sigma Theta, Inc, Sorors, especially my Delta Eta Line Sisters.

I want to thank Reverend Muriel Johnson and Reverend Dr. Martha Simmons who helped me early on process my call. I am still working through your advice and assignments.

I want to thank Reverend Adrianne Phillips, Reverend Yani Davis, Carl W. Kenney II, Reverend Dr. Gregory K, Moss, Sr., Reverend Dr. Robert C. Scott, and Reverend Dr. Jeremiah A. Wright for your willingness to provide meaningful insights, edits, forewords, afterwords, and reviews of my work.

I want to thank my many friends who have supported my events and pushed me when I wanted to give up.

My loving family, my cousins, aunties, daughters (Da'Vyne Destini & Adesina Da'Light), my loving sister (Ramona), and my parents, you are truly the wind beneath my wings.

And, finally, I thank God for all of the many ways you have molded me for such a time as this.

About the Author

Deborah "d²" Dalton is a poet/spoken word artist, domestic and sexual abuse advocate and survivor, currently seeking to poetically share the divine revelations gained while engaged in worship, study, and prayer. She was born in St. Albans, Queens, New York. Being brought up in a military family, she had the opportunity to be raised all over the world. While enrolled in a pre-engineering program at the University of Arkansas at Pine Bluff, she was an active member of the John McLinn Ross Players and performed in the following plays: *The River Niger* (Wilhelmina Brown), *Tobacco Road* (Ada Lester), *Othello* (Desdemona), *A Raisin in the Sun* (Beneatha Younger), *Aladdin's Lamp* (Mother), *Fences* (Rose Maxson), and *The Shadow Box* (Beverly). She received an Irene Ryan Acting Award Nomination and an Acting Achievement Award in the Southwest Collegian Regional Competition. She received her degree in Mechanical Engineering from Prairie View A&M University. After working for 15+ years in the construction industry in various project management and design functions, she decided to commit full-time to her calling to engage in ministry.

Other Published Works

Becoming Aware, 1998, 2000
A Mother's Solace - Healing Words, 2015
Strawberry Soda Water, A Chapbook, 2024

Contributor:
  The 2017 Poetry Marathon Anthology
  The 2019 Poetry Marathon Anthology
  The 2020 Poetry Marathon Anthology
  The 2021 Poetry Marathon Anthology
  The 2022 Poetry Marathon Anthology
  DIMEPIECE: Ten Years of CLI Poetry, 2023